The Entrepreneurial Region

And the Story of Medellín's Economic Transformation

Arnault Morisson

About the Author: Arnault Morisson has a PhD in Economic Geography from Utrecht University (Netherlands) and the Mediterranean University of Reggio Calabria (Italy). He has lived in Barcelona, Bogotá, Boston, Hanoï, Medellín, Milan, Paris, Prague, Reggio Calabria, São Paulo, Sydney, and Utrecht. He is passionate about making cities and regions more innovative and more interesting.

"This book is indispensable reading for policy makers and concerned citizens everywhere. We are living times for institutional innovation, when the regional and local levels are ideal spaces for experimentation. The successes and failures of others are the best source of lessons to enrich our own transformative efforts in these turbulent times."

Carlota Perez

Author of *Technological Revolutions and Financial Capital: the Dynamics of Bubbles and Golden Ages*

Contents

List of Figures, Map, and Tables

List of Acronyms

ACI	Agencia de Cooperación e Inversión de Medellín
ANDI	Asociación Nacional de Empresarios de Colombia
BCN	Bloque Cacique Nutibara
BITS	Building on Information Technology Strengths
CEDEZO	Centros de Desarrollo Empresarial Zonal
CEO	Chief Executive Officer
COMFAMA	Caja de Compensación Familiar de Antioquia
CONVIVIR	Servicios Especiales de Vigilancia y Seguriadad Privada
CTA	Centro de Ciencia y Tecnología de Antioquia
CUEE	Comité Universidad Empresa Estado
DARPA	Defense Advanced Research Projects Agency
DEA	Drug Enforcement Agency
ECLAC	United Nations Economic Commission for Latin America and the Caribbean
EDU	Empresa de Desarrollo Urbano
EDU	Empresa de Desarrollo Urbano
EEG	Evolutionary Economic Geography
ELN	Ejército de Liberación Nacional
ENIAC	Electronic Numerical Integrator And Computer
EPM	Empresas Públicas de Medellín
ESIF	European Structural and Investment Funds
EU	European Union
EURADA	European Association of Development Agencies
FARC-EP	Fuerzas Armadas Revolucionarias de Colombia— Ejército del Pueblo
FDI	Foreign Direct Investment

GDP	Gross Domestic Product
GEA	Grupo Empresarial Antioqueño
GPT	General Purpose Technology
HDI	Human Development Index
HP	Hewlett Packard
ICT	Information and Communication Technologies
IMF	International Monetary Fund
MIT	Massachusetts Institute of Technology
NEG	New Economic Geography
NGT	New Growth Theory
NSI	National System of Innovation
NTT	New Trade Theory
NYC	New York City
OCAD	Collegiate Bodies of Administration and Decision
OCyT	Observatorio Colombiano De Ciencia y Tecnología
OECD	Organisation for Economic Co-operation and Development
PCT	Patent Cooperation Treaty
PEPES	Perseguidos por Pablo Escobar
PMO	Project Management Office
PRIMED	Programa Integral de Mejoramiento de Barrios Informales
R&D	Research and Development
RDA	Regional Development Agency
RIA	Regional Innovation Agency
RIS	Regional Innovation System
RUEDA	Red Unificada de Emprendimiento de Antioquia
S3	Smart Specialization Strategy
SBIR	Small Business Innovation Research
SME	Small and Medium Enterprise
SMP	Sociedad de Mejoras Públicas
STEM	Science, Technology, Engineering, and Mathematics

STI	Science, Technology, and Innovation
STIF	Science, Technology and Innovation Fund
TRL	Technology Readiness Level
UN	United Nations
UNDP	United Nations Development Programme
US	United States
WSJ	Wall Street Journal

Acknowledgements

In 2013, I did an internship at Ruta N, Medellín's innovation agency. The Ruta N team shared with me their visions for the city, the region, and the Ruta N building complex. They wanted the city to become the most innovative city in Latin America by 2021, the region to become prosperous and full of opportunities for all, and the building complex to be full of startups and international companies, like Google. At the time, their propositions seemed quite unrealistic. The city was far from being the most innovative city in Latin America, the region was highly inequitable and violent, and the building complex was almost empty.

When I came back to Ruta N and Medellín in 2017, I found that the city had rapidly transformed itself. Medellín was becoming more innovative on different indicators, the regions had rapidly modernized, and the Ruta N building complex was full of startups and international companies. The propositions that seemed unrealistic in 2013 were now conceivable. Although Medellín is not yet the most innovative city in Latin America, its case shows that with the right leadership and a consistent strategy, cities can rapidly transform themselves in an extraordinary manner. This book tells the story of this transformation and provides a roadmap to emulate such transformation.

I am grateful to all the people I met during this journey who shared their experience and knowledge. In particular, I am grateful to the persons who took the time to write a Foreword. **Guillermo Dorronsoro** who emphasizes the role of political consistency and the importance of civil society for building regional innovation ecosystems. **Elkin Echeverrí** who argues that the concept of the Entrepreneurial Region can even be applied to regions on the knowledge core. **Marco Ferretti** who points out the importance of leadership for regional transformation. **Juan Pablo Ortega** who points out that cities are the most critical governance level to find solutions to complex problems. **Carlota Perez** who provides a great blurb. **Christian Saublens** who emphasizes the importance of public sector innovation to implement innovation strategies. **Elvira Uyarra** who stresses the importance of geography in tackling grand challenges.

Forewords.

Guillermo Dorronsoro, Former Manager of Innobasque

The creation of an innovation ecosystem is undoubtedly one of the keys to the prosperity of territories in this 21st century. From the perspective of my experience in the creation and consolidation of the Basque Innovation Agency—Innobasque—this book summarizes in a very appropriate way the keys to success of this type of initiatives. The leadership of public agents must be balanced with the participation of private agents, and with the construction of a science and technology infrastructure (public-private) that contributes to the promotion of the knowledge industry in the region

The foundations of this system have a lot to do with the educational model:

- A well-educated society, with informed and critical citizens, who are capable of understanding what must be changed to adapt to novel times, and what must be preserved to maintain roots and social cohesion.
- A structured and mobilized civil society that understands that future challenges require commitment, and not only request others (administrations or companies) to do the work.
- Leaders, in politics, in business, and in civil society, with the vision to make medium and long-term transformation bets, the courage to explain them to civil society and to carry them forward even if civil society does not fully understand them...

To these generic conditions, we must add three specific ones.

- To transform, new ideas are crucial. It has been a long time that we know that a good system of Science and Technology is the best way to produce them. Universities, Research Centers and Technological

Centers that are publishing on the frontier of human knowledge, guarantee companies a source of innovations always renewed.

- Of course, ideas can not remain in scientific publications, they have to reach companies and society. This requires creating an ecosystem that, based on basic research, is capable of applying it to technological developments and innovations that generate new products and services. The closer to the market, the less public funds are needed: private money enters quickly the closer research is to commercialization.
- We talked about the importance of investments in the previous points, because without gasoline the car does not travel far. But it is also not enough to have fuel: the engine has to work effectively. The R&D&I System requires good governance and continuous benchmarking with the best international standards to guarantee that public investments result in the best outcomes.

To develop such an innovation ecosystem, it takes two or three decades, not two or three years. Political elections should not alter the needed consistency and stability to build such innovation ecosystem as it is not good to lurch because it destroys what was created in previous years…

Elkin Echeverrí, Planning and Prospective Director at Ruta N Medellín

The Entrepreneurial Region shows us the importance of a new role of the state within regional ecosystems at the condition when the public sector can operate in an adequate and modern way in cities and their surrounding areas.

The future of the world lies in cities. Already, more than half of the world's population lives in cities. Not only do urban centers generate the problems that affect most people, but they also have the capacity to produce the most advanced solutions to respond to these challenges. As explained in this book, cities can be machines of innovation.

Despite the wide acceptance of these facts, most architects of public policy continue to propose generic systems at the national level without paying much attention to local contexts. This book can be an excellent starting guide for leaders around the world who do not want to settle for mainstream policies and who instead want to create new paths for their societies, regardless of whether they are peripheral, third world, emerging, in the Global South or part of whatever the often unfair and inaccurate designation one wants to apply.

This proposed new approach might well be applied to all cities around the world, even those in the knowledge "core." It is possible that most advanced innovation ecosystems do not realize this due to their past legacies and current status, but when they finally understand their need to act, it will probably be too late. I argue, without compromising the author, that this book can be valuable for the leaders of most advanced cities who do not want to have their cities live from a celebrated past but want to instead adapt to the present and prepare for a future that is accelerating every day and for everyone.

For readers, the economic framework used in this book is very useful for comparing to neo-classical economic development theories. The evolutionary approach, agglomeration economies, and neo-Schumpeterian theories are undoubtedly much closer to what regions need in building their knowledge-based economies, and they invite updating mainstream economists who still are very influential in thinking about economic development in most countries and regions.

I still remember with clarity and affection when the author first arrived in Medellín and worked on my team. Arnault was always scrutinizing everything in a rigorous and systematic manner. For several years, he has gone back and forth, compiling with great patience information and valuable knowledge of Medellín, of the ecosystem, and of Ruta N, which with his academic background and world experience make him an experienced and neutral observer, and someone who has given us many valuable pieces of advice to keep moving forward.

As the author correctly mentioned, Ruta N will always be "an element of policy running ahead of theory." The speed at which the city, the innovation ecosystem of Medellin, and Ruta N are changing fortunately show that Medellín continues to evolve at a great pace. This is why there already is the need for a new version of the book and a challenge for the author to write a second book.

Marco Ferretti, Full Professor at Parthenope University of Naples

In my experience as an academic, I have deepened the topic of *The Entrepreneurial Region* from different angles. In the mid 90s, I was fascinated by the studies of Anna Lee Saxenian describing the extraordinary dynamics concerning unique places as Silicon Valley and Route 128 where innovation proved to be able to drive regional economies by creating new jobs and higher standards of living for the local community. Later on, when these models of regional empowerment started to be questioned by the idea that "there is no one-size-fits-all " regional policy, especially in non-high tech regions, I felt the need to dedicate my studies to the dynamics of regional development in emergent regions.

From the empirical observation of regional development strategies in emerging countries, I learnt that there was often a main player undertaking a leadership role in the regional development, whether it be a large firm, a government institution or a large university.

By way of illustration, Acer Inc. played a key role in turning the province of Hsinchu (Taiwan) the hub of an innovation ecosystem - the *Asian Silicon Valley* - by building a supplier network of existing firms, and engaging in the creation of new ones to enrich the local system of SMEs. Conversely, in Iran it was the government to be directly engaged in the entrepreneurial development through policies to attract FDIs and make the economy less dependent on oil, as promoted by the Industrial Development and Renovation Organization (IDRO). Finally, the key role of the National University of Singapore (NUS) in the creation of the Singapore Biopolis, showed me the potential of the academic third mission of the university in driving local economies.

However, too much reliance upon top-down approaches through policies prioritizing investments in target sectors as well as putting the fate of entire regional economies in the hands of one large industrial player, has its own risks. For example, the presence of Alenia aeronautics in Campania showed the shortcomings associated to the embeddedness of an industry leader in a territory with a low entrepreneurial capacity. In fact, the creation a local supplier network of SMEs mainly engaged to address the specific demands of Alenia turned out to flatten the innovation capacity of the local firms and make them totally dependent on one single company.

At a later stage of my career, I felt the need to put the knowledge acquired during the years, to the service of my home region Campania (South of Italy). One of the initiatives in which I decided to take an active role is the Regional Entrepreneurship Acceleration Program (REAP) designed by the MIT which trains every year regional team leaders around the world to develop their own development strategy based on the regional competitive advantage. The MIT approach to regional development is based on the ecosystem framework and on the aim of developing both the entrepreneurship and innovation capacity of the region. My experience as a champion of the Team REAP Campania has re-shaped my idea of the entrepreneurial region, from a single actor-based view with a leadership role, to the need of adopting an ecosystem approach to the design of regional policies. By bringing around the table actors from different environments, as policy makers, entrepreneurs, academics and investors, I realized that a dialogue was not only possible, but also necessary to the design of effective interventions that would reflect the multi-dimensional nature of the regional competitiveness.

I find that this book describes very well this multi-dimensional view and offers a brilliant overview of the contemporary concept of the entrepreneurial region.

Juan Pablo Ortega, Co-founder and Former CEO of Ruta N

The 21st century is the century of cities. Large transformations are not coming from the initiatives of nation states, but instead from the cities that move forward in creating *glocal* solutions for the most important challenges of our time, such as climate change or the 4th industrial revolution.

In this crucial moment, *The Entrepreneurial Region* can help policymakers, innovation experts, implementers, and enthusiasts with a study of the most critical components for a city to pursue to foster social and economic development. There are no excuses as the knowledge, technology, and capabilities are spread and accessible; the lack of leadership and commitment will be the sole difference between cities that move forward and those that are left behind.

In Medellín, I was blessed to be part of the city's transformation, taking an active role of the process that the city followed in the last 15 years to become a Knowledge City: it started with the entrepreneurship policies that we put in place in 2004 at Ruta N, Medellín's innovation agency, and we are now starting initiatives to take advantage of the perfect "storm" that we have in place to join the 4th industrial revolution and the creative economy. This experience has taught me that any city has the capability and human talent to make the difference, and this book shows us the roadmap to do so.

Today, Medellín and most cities around the world have complex challenges, including air pollution, traffic congestion, insecurity, and inequality, but at the same time, they have the possibility to develop solutions that not only impact their citizens but also humanity as a whole. For Medellín, the recent announcement from the World Economic Forum to select the city as the home of the first 4th Industrial Revolution Center in a Spanish-speaking city in the world brings an immense opportunity to foster innovative approaches to solve those *glocal* challenges, solving local problems with global perspectives.

Christian Saublens, Former CEO of EURADA

***The Entrepreneurial Region*: myth or reality?** My experience working for more than 30 years for the European Association of Regions and Municipalities and for the European Association of Development Agencies (EURADA) tells me that there is a gap between rhetoric and practice in many regions in the field of entrepreneurship and innovation. The main reason lies in the fact that many policymakers in the European Union (EU) and management authorities of European Structural and Investment Funds (ESIF) focus on strategy rather than implementation.

How can we explain that almost all regions have put in place similar entrepreneurial boosters as those in Silicon Valley, Bangalore, or Boston without reaching their achievements? I believe that this is due to a lack of critical mass in terms of public human capital, private investors, and serial entrepreneurs on one hand, and to weak public sector agility, trust in intermediary organisations like regional development agencies (RDAs), and misunderstanding of the end users' needs on the other hand. There is a strong assumption that framework conditions create growth and the misperception between the notion of efficiency and effectiveness. Elected officials often put aside budget to create innovation infrastructures, such as incubators, technology centres, or science parks, without allocating the necessary funding for top managers, running costs, and updating of infrastructure. Politicians dream of creating a Silicon "something" when most often, companies need support to absorb knowledge to improve their products and services.

The concept of the entrepreneurial region cannot be dissociated from public sector innovations. The topic of innovation has been on the agenda of intermediary organisations and policymakers for many years, causing a real "innovate or die" dilemma. Their attentions have been focused on the provision of support services for entrepreneurs and enterprises, while little attention has been given to innovation inside those intermediary organizations and the public sector.

Moreover, when a public sector innovation is introduced, it is often a "copy paste" buzz concept rather than a tailored solution in response to an identified regional challenge. In many cases, the adopters have no access to the necessary human capital or funding to ensure the successful implementation of the innovation concept.

Last but not least, public entities are promoting innovation without being able to innovate themselves. One would expect public administrations advocating business innovation as a driver of regional development to be able to innovate in their own organisations, but this is seldom the case.

RDAs can appear as conservative organisations but shouldn't always take the blame. Indeed, they have to report to or seek permission from the regional and national administration, which is often "innovation adverse" for many reasons, including resistance to change, risk adversity, preference for the "business as usual" way of doing things, error-free culture, limiting regulatory/administrative frameworks, reporting to a pyramid authority/hierarchy based on seniority, few or no rewarding mechanisms, "not invented here syndrome," low regard for public administration...

Amongst the main limitations to innovation in the field of regional development are the EU legislations related to State Aid and public procurement, the national resistance to allow public organizations to charge for their services or their obligation to offer universal services instead of supporting the most "promising winners" or "hidden champions," and restrictions to manage financial instruments. Lastly, in some countries, there is a tradition to solve a problem by creating a new legal entity, which at the end of the day creates an unreadable map of intermediary organizations.

Elvira Uyarra, Associate Professor at The University of Manchester

In the last few years we have witnessed an upsurge of interest in so-called transformative (Schot & Steinmuller, 2018) and mission-oriented innovation policies (Mazzucato, 2018) seeking to direct innovation towards addressing grand challenges. Marianna Mazzucato has argued that addressing those challenges requires a confident "entrepreneurial state" able to take risks and "think big".

However geography is generally lacking in this policy agenda. A regional focus is important because innovation is spatially sticky and societal-challenges geographically diverse and contextual. Policies are also implemented locally, and rely on actors 'on the ground' with practical skills and knowledge of place-specific problems and the context in which their solution will have to be implemented.

The Entrepreneurial Region is therefore a welcome contribution to the debate on the entrepreneurial state. It highlights the pivotal role that regions play in innovation processes and the transformative potential of the public sector not just in developing countries but also in the Global South.

It is an engaging and well-researched book which masterfully combines evolutionary approaches of technical change with economic geography to explore the transformative role of the state. It documents the case of Ruta N, a fascinating account of institutional entrepreneurship driving the transformation of Medellin from a 'narco city' to a 'knowledge city'. From this case the author articulates a very useful roadmap or framework for regional innovation agencies in the 'knowledge periphery'.

This book should be recommended reading for students and researchers of local economic development, regional innovation systems and evolutionary economic geography. The book should also be of interest to policy-makers and practitioners interested in regional innovation policy and smart specialisation strategies.

Introduction.

In 2013, Mariana Mazzucato published her seminal book *The Entrepreneurial State* in which she shows the importance of state intervention in the economy to foster radical technological innovations (Mazzucato, 2013). The state, she says, has been behind every major technological innovations of the past century. Think of the Internet, biotechnology, robotics, or even every major component of the iPhone. Governments through various initiatives promote technological innovations either directly, the most famous example being the program Defense Advanced Research Projects Agency (DARPA) in the United States, or indirectly through massive tax-breaks and public procurements, of which Tesla and SpaceX are prime examples (Hirsch, 2015).

The idea that the state should intervene in the economy within a complex systemic approach to promote industrial development is not new. It can be traced back to Friedrich List, the German catch-up theorist, who pointed out that "in order to allow freedom of trade to operate naturally, the less advanced nation (Germany) must first be raised by artificial measures to that stage of cultivation to which the English nation has been artificially elevated" (List, 1856, p. 207). Tariffs can help protect infant industries until they can compete globally, such as the shipbuilding industry in South Korea (Chang, 2011). In China, the great firewall, which is an example of extreme digital protectionism, has facilitated large Chinese Internet companies, such as Alibaba, Tencent, and Baidu, reaching the critical mass and network effect to compete globally. Meanwhile in the European Union, French and German leaders are still wondering why Europeans don't have any large Internet companies. Instead of pointing the finger to failed industrial and digital policies, the culprit is apparently the European culture that is too risk averse for creating startups (Huuhtanen, 2015).

This does not mean that the state should constantly intervene to promote industrial development and become the main actor in the innovation process. The Soviet Union developed some interesting technological innovations, Sputnik being one of them (among many military projects), but ultimately failed because of a lack of "animal spirits" and an absence of individual entrepreneurs who understood how technological innovations could be turned into profitable business opportunities (Josephson, 1995). The Anglo-French state consortia designed and built the first commercial supersonic jet, the Concorde airplane, which was a great technological achievement but a commercial failure (Chittum, 2018). As a result, the role of the state must be that of a partner investing in fundamental research, mission-oriented innovations, and grand societal challenges that will take 20 to 30 years to become successful commercial products. In sum, the state must partner with the private sector to invest in risky and uncertain technological endeavors that private actors are unwilling to pursue alone.

This book applies the concept of the entrepreneurial state to the regional scale. The entrepreneurial state informs us that the state can be an essential actor in supporting the creation of disruptive and radical innovations. The entrepreneurial state has, however, two main shortcomings. First, it raises the question of the relevance of the concept for countries in the Global South. Do they really have the capabilities (either institutional, financial, or technological) to invest to support the next wave of disruptive technological innovations? Second, what about regions? Do they have any role to play in the innovation process? This book provides some answers to both of these questions.

The entrepreneurial region emphasizes the importance of the regional government partnering with the private sector to support regional structural change. It is ultimately at the regional scale, more specifically at the scale of the metropolitan-region, that the innovation process takes place. Patenting and research and development (R&D) activities concentrate in a few innovative regions around the world. In France and the United Kingdom for instance, Paris and London account for more than 40% of the country's total patent applications (OECD, 2006). We will see that there are strong evolutionary mechanisms that lock in regions into superior or inferior technological trajectories. Regions like Silicon

Valley, Tokyo, or London continuously transform themselves in an extraordinary manner while other regions face stagnation or decline. This book explores how regions can break the evolutionary mechanisms locking them into inferior technological trajectories and catch up technologically with regions in the knowledge core.

Regions have a fundamental role to play in promoting regional structural change. Their role is, however, both less ambitious and more complex at the same time compared to nation states. It is less ambitious, as it does not try to respond to grand societal challenges or to promote the next wave of disruptive technological innovations. It is more complex, as it involves many different dimensions. Indeed, innovation is non-linear and involves not only scientific and technological interactions but also local interactions among knowledge-driven structures, such as institutions and organizations or the socio-institutional structure. As a result, regions not only have to support the development of scientific and technological knowledge but also to promote institutional and organizational changes. Regions must support firms in acquiring scientific and technological capabilities, especially in the regions located in the Global South where firms have some difficulties in acquiring, absorbing, and exploiting scientific and technological knowledge. Additionally, regions must also affect the evolution of the socio-institutional structure with the novel techno-economic paradigm to ensure inclusive and shared economic growth.

Regions are, however, facing major difficulties in supporting this process of technological catch-up. Although they are the key to promote economic convergence, they are also prone to a lack of institutional capabilities and rampant corruption. In the European Union, the European Commission dedicated €351.8 billion for the programming period 2014-20 under the EU Cohesion Policy to promote convergence among regions in the European Union with little success (European Commission, 2018a). The expertise brought by the European Commission and their massive resources did little to counter the low quality of government, the low institutional capabilities, and the lack of capacity to absorb funds of some regions in the European Union (See Charron, Dijkstra, & Lapuente, 2014; Farole, Rodriguez-Pose, & Storper, 2011; Oughton, Landabaso, & Morgan, 2002). The South of Italy has received significant funding within the EU Cohesion Policy and spent most of that which didn't line the pockets of Mafias in an unstainable manner. In Naples, which is a great example of mismanagement, €720,000 of the EU Cohesion Fund were used to pay for an Elton John concert in 2009 (BBC, 2010).

For unorthodox neo-Schumpeterian economists, like myself, innovation is central for economic growth and to increasing standards of living. In the European Union, the divergence between core and peripheral regions is due to the divergence of innovation intensity. Between 2001 and 2013, the only region in France that has grown above the GDP national average is the region of Ile de France where Paris is located (Iammarino, Rodríguez-Pose, & Storper, 2017). This is not an isolated case but a recurrent pattern among all the countries in the European Union. Technological and scientific knowledge are localized, which explains this process of economic divergence between regions. Mainstream neo-classical economists have little to say about the innovation process (See Rosenberg, 1982). They see it as a "black box."

Neoliberal ideas or theories for promoting economic development in the Global South have consistently failed, and for good reasons. Consciously or unconsciously, they were promoting Western economic interests and hindering the long-term economic development that would have jeopardized those interests. The "shock therapy" in Russia after the fall of the Soviet Union or the IMF-sponsored "Washington consensus" that consisted in limiting the role of the state and laissez-faire economic reforms are good examples of ill-fated neoliberal reforms (Murrell, 1993). In Latin America, the "Washington consensus" resulted in a lost decade with little to no growth for the Latin American countries that most vigorously reformed their countries, of which Argentina is a good example (Rodrik, 2006). Neoliberal economists will, however, rationalized their failures in conceptualizing economic development by arguing that Latin America's lost decade was due to timidity in privatizing and promoting laissez-faire markets (Williamson, 2002).

In investigating the failure of neoliberal reforms in Latin America and the economic success of East Asian countries where governments have played a major role in transforming their economies, Dani Rodrik (2008), the famous Harvard University professor in political economy, proposes a renewed role for the state in supporting the innovation process. As for every aspect of life, the best recipe for reforming countries or regions to promote economic development is moderation. Both the market and the state are important and both should be strong and efficient to balance the other. Which should be the stronger is a matter that I leave to neoliberal and Marxist ideologues. The proposition to promote an "entrepreneurial state" has resonated well in Colombia, and particularly in Medellín, which has followed a post-Washington consensus approach to local economic development (Bateman, Duran Ortíz, & Maclean, 2010). Since 2004, the city of Medellín has conducted reforms in social inclusion, social urbanism, education, transportation, and innovation to transform itself into a knowledge city. At the center of the innovation strategy is the regional innovation agency Ruta N. This book will contextualize the theories of *The Entrepreneurial Region* into the specific case of Medellín and its innovation agency Ruta N.

This book includes three main parts. The first part introduces the concept of *The Entrepreneurial Region*. The second part presents Medellín in Colombia as a case study of an Entrepreneurial Region. The case study provides a rich description of the regional institutional context, the actors, and Ruta N, the regional innovation agency behind Medellín's economic transformation. Lastly, the book provides a toolkit for regional policymakers to stimulate regional structural change in a sustainable and inclusive manner. Most often, books that present an argument tend to move from facts to theories, from theories to conjectures, from conjectures to opinions, from opinions to pure ideology and from ideology back to facts. The lack of demarcations is usually because books are often too ambitious and repeat over and over again the same argument in a different way. This book merges facts and theories with empirical evidence to provide a more complete picture of what The Entrepreneurial Region is. The adoption of the concept of The Entrepreneurial Region ultimately rests in the hands of regional policymakers and actors who must possess the willingness, the opportunity, the motivation, and the capabilities to transform their regions.

Part I

The Concept of
The Entrepreneurial Region

CHAPTER 1

The Knowledge Economy and Regional Divergence.

Policymakers put regional innovation policies at the top of their policy agendas, viewing innovation as a panacea that "provides the foundation for new businesses, new jobs, and productivity growth and is thus, an important driver of economic growth and development" (OECD, 2015a, p. 13). Technological innovation drives productivity growth as well as the quality and quantity of jobs, which are critical to improve standards of living (OECD, 2011a). Indeed, technological innovation is considered to be a dominant force in economic growth. In a post-2008 era characterized by low economic growth, innovation is seen as a transformative force for developed and developing economies with the capacity to address pressing social and global challenges, such as demographic shifts, resource scarcity, and climate change, while supporting more productive, resilient, and higher-income economies (Metcalfe & Ramlogan, 2008).

We know from the work of Cobb and Douglas (1928) and Solow (1957) that there are only two ways of increasing the output of the economy: an economy can either increase the number of inputs that go into the productive process, which include land, labor, and capital, or an economy can innovate ways to get more output from the same number of inputs. The impact of technical progress on economic growth was first synthesized into a coherent empirical whole by Solow (1957) from the work of Abramovitz (1956) who measured the growth of the output and the growth of the inputs of the American economy between 1870 and 1950. Solow used a modified production function, $Y=f(K, L, t)$, in which K is capital, L is labor, and t represents technical change over time. The measured growth of inputs (i.e., in capital and labor) accounted for about 15% of the actual growth in the output of the economy, and 85% was an unexplained statistical residual, in other words, technical change. He discovered that technical change accounted for 87.5% of economic growth when deriving estimates of the United States total factor productivity between 1909 and 1949. Although later works have debated the actual residual contribution to economic growth, it is taken as axiomatic that innovation is the single, most important, component of long-term economic growth.

Economic growth, however, as economists knew it, might be over. Indeed, perpetual economic growth is an extrapolation from history and a pious hope for the future, not a law of nature (Ayres, 2006). There are many drivers of past growth in industrialized countries that are now showing signs of saturation or exhaustion. Growth optimists argue that technological change, especially in emerging sectors, such as artificial intelligence, information technology, nanotechnology, biotechnology, and robotics, can secure a lasting high economic growth. The driver for technological innovations and economic growth are General Purpose Technologies (GPT). These are pervasive technologies—such as the electricity or information and communication technologies (ICT)—spread to many sectors, having a high rate of improvement, making it easier to invent or produce other innovations, and affecting the entire economy. As discovered by Kondratieff (1984) and later supported by Schumpeter (1939), the occurrence of major technological transitions is associated with the cycle of economic expansion, which allows the process of creative destruction to take place.

The economy is going through successive phases of development, also referred to as cycles or waves, that simultaneously occur with the introduction of breakthrough technologies or General Purpose Technology. According to Gordon (2012), there have been three industrial revolutions. The First Industrial Revolution, which spanned from 1750 to 1830, was triggered by the invention of the steam engine and railroads. The Second Industrial Revolution, which lasted from 1870 to 1900, made mass-production possible with discoveries and advancements in the use of electricity, the internal combustion engine, running water, indoor plumbing, communications, entertainment, chemicals, and petroleum. The Third Industrial Revolution, which began in the 1960s, was centered around the diffusion of microelectronics, building on the sequential discoveries of the transistor (1947), the integrated circuit (1957), the planar process (1959), semiconductors (1960s), the microprocessor (1971), the personal computers (1970s and 1980s), the Internet (1990s), and smartphones (2000s). The Third Industrial Revolution, which was triggered by Information Communication Technologies (ICTs), reached its peak in the dot.com era of the late 1990s. Two unique features characterize the Third Industrial Revolution. First, knowledge is the fundamental feature of the third industrial revolution. While information and knowledge have been two essential features of every industrial revolution, the difference with the latest is that "information and knowledge are not only its raw materials but also its outcomes" (Castells, 1994, p. 13). Some authors believe that the world is at the commencement of a fourth industrial revolution (see Schwab, 2016). The Fourth Industrial Revolution is "characterized by a much more ubiquitous and mobile internet, by smaller and more powerful sensors that have become cheaper, and by artificial intelligence and machine learning" (Schwab, 2016, p. 7).

The Third Industrial Revolution has been dubbed the "knowledge-based economy" in which capitalist economies are transitioning towards a "post-Fordist," "post-industrial," or "post-modern" economy (Drucker, 1994). The transition is characterized by the emergence of technological, market, social, and institutional forces markedly different from those which dominated the economy after the Second World War (Amin, 1994, p. 1). Although, technology and knowledge are closely interrelated since technology is defined as "the use of scientific knowledge to specify ways of doing things in a reproducible manner," knowledge in the knowledge-based economy is paramount since "knowledge feeds upon knowledge itself in order to generate higher productivity" (Castells, 1994, p. 10). The knowledge-based economy is characterized by increasing returns to scale (Arthur, 1996). Indeed, knowledge is different from other inputs of production in that it is extremely durable, its use does not reduce its stock, and in fact its use often creates new knowledge. Indeed, knowledge can be repeatedly without reducing its stock. The increasing return to scale nature of knowledge does not generate equilibrium but instability. Indeed, as shown by Arthur (1996, p. 100) "if a product or a company or a technology—one of many competing in a market—gets ahead by chance or clever strategy, increasing returns can magnify this advantage, and the product or company or technology can go on to lock-in the market." Increasing properties are characterized by market instability, multiple potential outcomes, unpredictability, market lock-in, possible inferior technological outcomes, and a winner-takes-all economy.

The Third Industrial Revolution, as with previous industrial revolutions, is characterized by the process of creative destruction (Schumpeter, 1939). Many academics argue, however, that this latest transition is different, and that jobs are being destroyed at a much faster rate than the creation of new jobs (see Brynjolfsson & McAfee, 2014). Indeed, the advent of the Internet, the ubiquitousness of software, automation, and information and communication technologies have profoundly transcended society and the labor market. Developed countries are confronted with an increase in non-standard employments and jobs polarization in the labor market, which is characterized by an increasing demand for both high-skilled and low-skilled jobs and a "hollowing out" in middle-skilled ones (Brynjolfsson & McAfee 2014). Non-standard employment, which includes: self-employment, temporary or fixed-term contracts, and part-time work, represents one-third of total employment in the OECD countries (OECD, 2015b). In the knowledge-based economy, work ethics have evolved to emphasize the importance of passion, freedom, and the pursuit of meaningful projects, blurring the boundaries between leisure and work (Himanen, 2010). At the same time, wealth distribution is increasingly skewed towards the superstars; people who dominate the activities in which they engage in, contributing to a winner-takes-all economy (Rosen, 1981).

The knowledge-based economy is not only a multidisciplinary academic concept but also a policy concept. The academic interest for innovation studies came into being in the 1980s and 1990s, at a time where developed countries experienced increased competition from low-cost-labor emerging countries due to the process of globalization (Freeman & Soete, 2004). Innovation studies aimed to conciliate the process of globalization with the theory of comparative advantage. Developed countries could, as a result, continue to enjoy high-growth rates and high-income per capita by moving up to higher value-added activities through innovation due to the nature of knowledge (Maskell & Malmberg, 1999a). The increased policy recognition of technological innovations as the primary determinant for long-term international competitiveness and trade performance has reduced "the economist's cartel argument in support of all trade liberalization" (Freeman & Soete, 2004, p. 334). Developed and emerging countries are, as a result, in an innovation race. In this race, China is transitioning rapidly into a knowledge-based economy compared to other developed and developing economies (Zhou & Leydesdorff, 2006). European countries are lagging behind the United States in producing technological innovations. Although the European Union countries are leading in top-level scientific outputs compared to the United States, they have not been able to transform these outputs into wealth-generating innovations. Dosi, Llerena, and Labini (2006) argue that this "European Paradox" is due to a weaker system of scientific research and a lower capacity for the European Union's innovative companies to transform scientific outputs into successful technological innovations.

Neoclassical growth theory assumes that technical change is exogenous and proceeds at a steady state. This is the so-called "manna from heaven" view of technology, where technology is a public good, accessible by all and at any time (Cameron, 1996). Science and technology is approached for neoclassical economists as a "black box" (Rosenberg, 1982). Neoclassical theories have, as a result, little to contribute in the understanding of technological innovations. However, neoclassical thoughts are so pervasive in economic life and in guiding government interventions that they require some discussion. The traditional neoclassical growth theory suggests that per-capita growth rates should be inversely related to initial levels of income (Solow, 1956). The neoclassical model incorporates labor and capital mobility in regional development, to the extent that, given identical production functions in all regions, labor will flow from low-wage to high-wage regions, and capital will flow in the opposite direction (Barro & Sala-i-Martin, 1992). The neoclassical model assumes that over time wages and growth will be the same between regions within the same country. The theory implies that income levels and growth rates of national economies and regional economies should converge over time.

The theory on convergence between regions has not shown to be consistent with the facts (Islam, 2003). The long-run growth indicates divergence in productivity and income between the richest and poorest countries since the industrial revolution (Landes, 1998). The clear predictive limitations of the neoclassical growth theory led to the emergence of several theories, such as New Growth Theory (NGT), New Trade Theory (NTT), and New Economic Geography (NEG), to correct these limitations. Rather than being exogenous, the endogenous growth theory attempted to endogenize the role of innovation in the growth process. Learning by doing, investment capital, human capital, infrastructure, or R&D are thus some of the determinants of technical change that are being incorporated in the growth model to better reflect the reality of the innovation process (see Amable, 1993; Romer, 1994). Increasing returns to scale and knowledge externalities make continuous growth and productivity growth possible. The endogenous growth theory, however, lacks in capturing organizational change or the relationships between institutional, technical, and investment change. The theory does not explain how technological innovation emerges and how it affects economic growth and development. The endogenous growth theories demonstrate that differences in production structures arise because of differences in underlying characteristics without explaining why those characteristics appear in the first place. We will see later that unorthodox economic theories, such as evolutionary economics, are much more helpful in understanding the innovation process.

The realization of the importance of the regional dimension in the process of innovation comes from the numerous case studies of regional divergence within the same countries, with the Third Italy versus the South of Italy, Baden-Württemberg (Germany), Haute-Savoie (France), Cambridge (United Kingdom), Regional Triangle Park (United States), or Silicon Valley versus Route 128 in Boston (Bagnasco, 1977; Saxenian, 1994). Success stories of highly specialized industrial agglomerations and clusters of regionally concentrated networks of Small and Medium Enterprises (SMEs) also significantly contributed to foster the interests of policymakers and scholars on regions as engines for growth and innovations. There is an economic divergence not only between widely historically disparate metropolitan-regions, such as North-South Italy but also between successful metropolitan-regions, such as Los Angeles and San Francisco. In the past decades, while Los Angeles has experienced the loss of its aerospace industry, a rise in low-skilled immigrants from Latin America, and government failure, San Francisco has become the technology innovation center of the information age (Storper, Kemeny, Makarem, & Osman, 2015). In the European Union, while there is a trend towards long-term convergence in productivity and income at the national level, regional-level analyses show a trend towards divergence within countries despite the efforts of EU Cohesion Policy to address this issue in different programming periods (Iammarino, Rodríguez-Pose, & Storper, 2017). We will see in the next chapter that regional divergence is mostly the outcome of the differences in regional innovative capacities due to the nature of technological innovations (Akcigit, Grigsby, & Nicholas, 2017).

This process of divergence between regions is highly worrying for three reasons. First, it not only creates divergence between regions but also within regions. San Francisco and Silicon Valley are not only the world center of the knowledge economy but also a highly unequal region. With a GINI Index of 51.48, the San Francisco County has one of the most unequal wealth distribution in the world (U.S. Census, 2018). Income inequality is bad but the social ills it creates are even worse. San Francisco is home to many drug addicts and homeless people who are called the "living dead" by the tech elite who live in multi-million-dollar apartments a few blocks away from the dirtiest block in the city (Fuller,

2018). Second, this concentration of wealth leads to resentment from regions on the periphery that are increasingly diverging from the innovation hubs. This resentment is leading to what Andrés Rodríguez-Pose refers to *"The Revenge of the Places that Don't Matter"* where people on the periphery increasingly vote for populist parties against the cosmopolitan elites living in regions in the knowledge core. Think of Brexit in the United Kingdom, Trump in the United States, the Gilets Jaunes in France, or Salvini in Italy (Rodríguez-Pose, 2018). Third, it reinforces power structure through feedback loops, limits social mobility, and concentrates wealth to unprecedented levels. Indeed, it is increasingly difficult for a person without inherited wealth to move to live and work in the places where wealth is created and accumulated, such as New York, San Francisco, Paris, or London, due to prohibitive housing prices, which is producing superstar regions where only the multi-millionaires can afford to live in (Florida, 2017; Goodman & Mayer, 2018). The issue of income inequality is not being addressed and not really debated as it should be. In a classic divide and conquer, the super-rich from New York City and the Silicon Valley are pushing multiple dimensions of inequality to dodge the debate on income inequality, ironically fuelling the beast of populism that they are trying to tame (See Freeland, 2012).

CHAPTER 2

Regions are Innovation Machines.

The economic divergence between regions within countries can seem surprising and paradoxical in a world that seems flatter thanks to information communication technologies (ICT). For many academics and pundits, the world was going to be flat thanks to ICT and the globalization process leading to the end of geography and the death of distance (See Cairncross, 1997; Friedman, 2005; O'Brien, 1992). Despite the increased mobility of goods, labor, capital, and knowledge, the flat world scenario has not occurred. In fact, ICT and globalization have greatly contributed to concentrate wealth, economic activities, financial flows, and innovative capacities in a few global metropolitan-regions (Rodríguez-Pose, & Crescenzi, 2008a; Sassen, 2001). Between 2011 and 2015, there were 950,000 patents filled in the world under the Patent Cooperation Treaty (PCT) of which the top 100 metropolitan-regions around the world accounted for 59 percent of all PCT filings (Bergquist, Fink, & Raffo, 2017). The region of Tokyo-Yokohama in Japan ranked first in the world with 94,079 patents filled between 2011-2015, followed by Shenzhen-Hong-Kong with 41,218 patents, and San Jose-San Francisco with 34,324 patents. The top three biggest regions represented 17.9 percent of the total patenting activity in the world while representing approximately 1% of the world population (Bergquist, Fink, & Raffo, 2017).

The concentration of technological innovations in a few metropolitan regions around the world is due to the cumulative, localized, tacit, and partly appropriable nature of scientific and technological knowledge. These mechanisms are the building blocks of the economic geography discipline, which emerged from the observations of the British economist Alfred Marshall (1890) who introduced the concept of agglomeration economies in his seminal book, *The Principles of Economics*. The concept of agglomeration economies is a form of external economies, which can be defined as services or disservices rendered without compensation by one producer to another one. External economies, or agglomeration economies, exist when a firm located in a specific urban environment has an enhanced productivity (Rosenthal & Strange, 2005).

Marshall suggests that agglomeration economies can be classified into three categories, those arising: from labor market interactions, which allow better matching between an employer and a worker; from linkages between intermediate- and final- goods suppliers, which enable internal increasing returns; and from knowledge spillovers, which allows for workers to learn from each other. External economies are crucial in understanding the process of cumulative causation and some principles in evolutionary economics, such as lock-in effects and self-reinforcing principles. Agglomeration economies involve a mechanism of cumulative causation, which suggests that an initial advantage can cause a lock-in effect generating further growth and multiplier effects (Myrdal, 1957). Agglomeration economies and cumulative causation suggest that the diffusion of new technologies are first adopted in larger and richer cities. Knowledge, skills, and capital, once acquired, do not vanish, but become an endogenous source of future endowments (Malecki, 1997).

Agglomeration economies are the sources of increasing returns to scale and of the reduction of firms' average cost of productions (Rosenthal & Strange, 2004). The advantages for firms locating in metropolitan-regions result from agglomeration economies, which allow them to generate higher productivity, wages, technological capabilities, and profits (Carlino, 1982). Knowledge-based companies tend to geographically concentrate in specific metropolitan-regions, which are thus innovation powerhouses. In the OECD countries, more than 81% of patents are filed by applicants located in metropolitan-regions (OECD, 2006). In Ireland, Greece, Finland, the Netherlands, Japan, Korea and Canada, a single metropolitan-region generates almost half of the national patenting activity (OECD, 2006). In France and the United Kingdom, Paris and London account for more than 40% of the country's total patent applications (OECD, 2006).

There are two types of knowledge spillovers: pure knowledge spillovers or non-pecuniary spillovers, and pecuniary spillovers. Pure knowledge spillovers are positive externalities, in which knowledge flows between adjacent producers and/or users of innovation, that occur without monetary transactions. In the case of pure knowledge spillovers, knowledge created by one agent can be used by another either without compensation or with compensation that is less costly than the value of the knowledge. Pure knowledge spillovers, which can be defined as a spatial public good, are knowledge that leak to other economic agents, thus generating positive externalities and fostering innovative activities. The mobility of highly-skilled workers, for instance, represents a strong mechanism for knowledge spillovers. In contrast, a pecuniary knowledge spillover occurs through monetary transaction, for instance, when one firm purchases R&D inputs or capital equipment.

Knowledge spillovers—that is, the knowledge created in one firm but used by another without pecuniary compensation—occur because knowledge is not a normal good. It is, for a large part, a non-rival and non-excludable good. Knowledge, due to its non-rival and non-excludable characteristics, can potentially be diffused rapidly between regions and between countries. The neoclassical interpretation even considers knowledge to be a "public good," that is, a good that is non-excludable and non-rival; and, as such, is accessible for everybody free of charge. Private firms aim, however, to maximize the rents from technological innovation through appropriability mechanisms. Appropriability refers to the tools and strategies that allow a firm to protect technological innovations, to varying degrees, as rent-yielding assets against imitation from its competitors. Dosi (1988) lists (a) patents, (b) secrecy, (c) lead times, and (d) costs required for duplication, (e) learning-curve effects, and (f) superior sales and services efforts, as appropriability devices. As a result, the properties of technological knowledge, of markets, and of the legal environment, favor and protect, to varying degrees, technological innovations.

Knowledge spillovers have some specific features, such as their spatial concentration, their decaying nature with distance, their lead time to leak to other firms, and their tendency to be enhanced with density. In regions in the European Union, knowledge spillovers are not traveling more than a 200 kilometers radius from the largest and most dynamic metropolitan-regions (Moreno, Paci, & Usai, 2005). Proximity affects the intensity of knowledge spillovers. It is widely agreed in the academic literature that proximity has a positive impact on learning, knowledge creation, and innovation. Proximity is especially important for knowledge-based industries where tacit knowledge plays a fundamental role in the generation of innovative activities, which appears to be at the early stages of the industry life cycle (Audretsch & Feldman, 1996). The concept of proximity has been developed in the 1990s by a French research group of economists and sociologists, to investigate the process of industrial agglomeration, such as an industrial district, technology park, or "innovative milieu" (Gilly & Torre, 2000). Building on the work of Gilly and Torre, Boschma (2005) distinguishes between five dimensions of proximity: cognitive, organizational, social, institutional, and geographical proximity. Boschma suggests that for each dimension of proximity, there exists an optimal state, between too little and too much proximity, that provides the best innovation outcomes.

Proximity facilitates knowledge spillovers due to the specific nature of knowledge. In his book, *The Tacit Dimension*, Michael Polanyi (1966) disseminates the concept of tacit knowledge, when he observes: "We can know more than we can tell... The skill of a driver cannot be replaced by a thorough schooling in the theory of the motorcar; the knowledge I have of my own body differs altogether from the knowledge of its physiology" (p. 4). The tacit dimension of knowledge is a component of human knowledge distinct from, but complementary to, codified knowledge (Polanyi, 1966). Tacit knowledge refers to the knowledge, ideas, concepts, shared beliefs, skills, competences, or insights that individuals possess, but which cannot be fully expressed since tacit knowledge is ill-defined, context-dependent, uncodified, unpublished, yet can, nonetheless, be to some extent shared with collaborators and colleagues who have a common experience. Tacit knowledge is most easily exchanged through repeated face-to-face interactions. The sense of local buzz within a region, that is "the information and communication ecology created by face-to-face contacts, co-presence and co-location of people and firms within the same industry and place or region", can facilitate the exchange and spread of tacit knowledge (Bathelt, Malmberg, & Maskell, 2004). In each technology, there is an element of tacitness that can only be interpreted internally due to cumulatively augmented abilities and skills. Tacit knowledge cannot be easily written down in a "blueprint" (and therefore easily diffused), either in the form of public or proprietary information. In contrast to tacit knowledge, codified knowledge consists of information and facts that can be expressed in various forms such as codes, standards, and rules, which, as a result, can be rapidly disseminated around the world.

One of the most important characteristics of tacit knowledge is its localized nature. Indeed, tacit knowledge is person-embodied and context-dependent, making it spatially sticky (Von Hippel, 1994). Knowledge or information is "sticky" when that knowledge or information is costly to acquire, transfer, and use. Due to the localized nature of tacit knowledge, it frequently enters the debate of government expenditures in public policies for science, technology, and innovation (Cowan, David, & Foray, 2000). The frequent argument against public expenditure to support science is that foreign companies would free-ride the knowledge generated, since information can freely flow between countries through the publications of basic discoveries in scientific journals. While this argument is to some extent applicable to codified knowledge, it does not apply to tacit knowledge. Indeed, tacit knowledge is sticky information and is central to strategic innovation policies for the development of countries, regions, or cities. Tacit knowledge does not travel freely. It resides in the heads of the engineers, scientists, and knowledge workers possessing it. The inherent stickiness of tacit knowledge allows firms and organizations to protect and appropriate the benefits deriving from research investments, at the condition of controlling the access to knowledge. Maskell and Malmberg (1999b) refer to the concept of ubiquitification to describe the process of mass codification of previously tacit knowledge in an increasingly globalized world. The process of ubiquitification "tends to undermine the competitiveness of firms in the high-cost areas of the world" that rely on codified or easily codified knowledge. More tacit forms of knowledge are thus even more critical today for sustaining a competitive advantage.

Information and Communication Technologies (ICTs) facilitate the codification of knowledge, which has an impact on the job market. The Polanyi's paradox, referring to the polarization of the labor market (which is the simultaneous growth of high-education, high-wage and low-education, low-wage jobs) can be explained because of the differences between tacit and codified knowledge (Autor, 2014). Indeed, computers rely on the skills of software developers to write successful programs. The job of a software developer is to meticulously codify knowledge into a series of steps required for the computer to perform a task. Autor shows that tacit knowledge is problematic to code into computer programs, especially when software programmers don't know the rules. While computers have been able to perform increasingly complex cognitive tasks due to the rapid advances in computer technology, they have been maladroit at mimicking human interactions. Deming (2015) argues that individuals with high levels of social and cognitive skills are being increasingly rewarded in the labor market.

In a recent study, Frey and Osborne (2017) estimate that the rapid developments in computer technology could put in jeopardy 47 percent of total U.S. employment in the next decade. Automation, the rapid development in software and ICT could even impact highly-skilled workers performing relatively tacit and non-routine tasks. In *The Second Machine Age*, Brynjolfsson and McAfee (2014) take the example of driving, which was once supposed to be impossible to automate, yet is now a reality. There has been little or no employment growth in high-paying jobs since 2000 (Acemoglu & Autor 2011). Indeed, Beaudry, Green, and Sand (2013) argue that there is even a "great reversal" in the demand for cognitive skill that began in the U.S. labor market in 2000 due to rapid advances in ICT that are redefining the meaning of routine jobs.

The concentration of technological innovations in a relatively small number of metropolitan-regions results from the nature of scientific and technological knowledge for five reasons. First, regions need to reach a certain threshold in scientific and technological knowledge to trigger the "principle of interlocking, circular inter-dependence within a process of cumulative causation" (Myrdal, 1957, p. 23). Second, the tacit nature of scientific and technological knowledge makes them sticky. Third, some level of proximity on multiple dimensions is needed to efficiently exploit scientific and technological knowledge. Fourth, metropolitan-regions are heterogeneous in absorbing and exploiting external knowledge (Audretsch & Feldman, 1996). Fifth, there is a spatial dimension of knowledge spillovers that limits the development of regions on the knowledge periphery (Rodríguez-Pose, & Crescenzi, 2008b).

CHAPTER 3

Evolutionary Economics for Regional Economic Development.

Neoclassical economics has a limited interest for policymakers designing innovation policies since they single out the institutional structure of the research systems of advanced industrial economies. Innovation is treated as a "black box" whose characteristics and internal processes are ignored. Nelson and Winter (1982) introduce the evolutionary economic perspective, which encompasses concepts from evolutionary biology and Schumpeterian economic thoughts. Evolutionary economics is the response to the limitations of neoclassical economics in explaining economic growth, technological change, technological evolution, the nature of competition and the role of institutions and routines in guiding individual behavior. In evolutionary economics, the nature of the economic problem is fundamentally different from neoclassical economics since "the set of choices are not given and the consequences of any choice are unknown" (Nelson & Winter, 1982, p. 276).

From an evolutionary perspective, technological change can be interpreted as "an irreversible, path-dependent and evolutionary process, stemming from the behavior of economic agents which explore only a limited part of the set of theoretically possible actions, that part which is strictly linked to previous innovation adoptions and to already acquired know-how" (Camagni, 1991, p. 125). The idea that economics should integrate evolutionary models first originated from Thorstein Veblen (1898), when he wrote an article asking "Why is Economics not an Evolutionary Science?" since in his view, evolutionary theories could integrate both continuity and change, both inertia and novelty and thus, better understand the complexity of the economic reality.

The evolutionary economic perspective merges concepts from the Schumpeterian growth models and evolutionary biology. The evolutionary economic paradigm could also be called "neo-Schumpeterian" since it encompasses the Schumpeterian growth model assumptions, such as that long-term growth is the result of innovation, that innovation is the result of investments, and that innovation triggers the phenomenon of creative destruction (Aghion & Howitt, 1990). For evolutionary economists, technological change is better interpreted with concepts coming from evolutionary biology, namely Darwinian and Lamarckian theories of evolution, rather than with concepts emanating from neoclassical economics. The two main theories of evolution come from Jean-Baptiste Lamarck and Charles Darwin, two 19th century biologists, who respectively published, *Philosophie Zoologique* and *On the Origin of Species*. Lamarckism emphasizes the idea that evolution is the outcome of "non-randomly acquired, beneficial phenotypic changes" that are inheritable. In contrast, Darwinism suggests the importance of "random, undirected change that provided material for natural selection" (Koonin & Wolf, 2009).

In Darwinism, adaptation, mutation, and variety occur across several generations. Socio-economic adaptation, mutation, and variety, however, can occur more rapidly, oftentimes within a lifetime. Although Lamarckism has largely been discredited in evolutionary biology, in evolutionary economics, both Lamarckism and Darwinism are important theories to explain technological change. In evolutionary economics, Lamarckism implies the importance of the process of learning and of the cumulative nature of innovation. Learning can be inherited since it can be seen as a process that can be passed on to future or other entities. In evolutionary economics, Darwinism implies variety, chance, novelty, mutation, adaptation, selection, accumulation, path-dependency, and retention. Nelson and Winter (1982) introduce three basic concepts of evolutionary economics. First, the concept of routine. Second, the concept of search to evaluate and replace routines. Third, the selection environment that is partly determined by conditions outside the firms in the industry or sector being considered.

The concepts developed in evolutionary economics are especially valuable in regional science for understanding the process of regional divergence. Boschma and Frenken (2006) introduce the concept of evolutionary economic geography (EEG) to analyze how spatial structures emerge from the micro-behavior of individuals and firms. Evolutionary concepts such as path dependency, routines, chance, increasing returns, and lock-in can generate regional divergence and diversity, which tend to persist over time due to the process of cumulative causation. The evolutionary approach is highly relevant in explaining the process of localized "collective" learning in a regional context, the adjustment problems that regions may be confronted with in a world of increasing variation, and the spatial formation of newly emerging industries as an evolutionary process in which the spatial connotation of increasing returns may result in a spatial lock-in. Additionally, historical events, historical accidents, and genius entrepreneurs can serve as catalysts in regional development. Scientific and technological knowledge is mutually dependent, self-reinforcing, and cumulative in nature. These features create path-dependency, which propel regions into inferior or superior technological trajectories. The EEG approach has made significant progress in understanding how new economic activities emerge with the concept of economic relatedness. From the work of Hidalgo, Klinger, Barabási, and Hausmann (2007) in the product space, the concept of economic relatedness points out that new regional activities or new industrial path developments are going to branch out from existing technologically-related regional industrial activities (Boschma, Minondo, & Navarro, 2013; Neffke, Henning, & Boschma, 2011). In other words, industries related to the existing industries in the region are more likely to emerge.

Boschma and van der Knaap (1997) point out that due to the discontinuous nature of radical innovations, the location of new industries can emerge in a window of locational opportunity or chance, which triggers path dependency and cumulative self-reinforcing feedback loops, which lead to the formation of a cluster. Chance can thus be the trigger of industrial clustering in specific regions due to the evolutionary nature of spatial development. A chance factor, such as the appointment of Fred Terman as the dean of the School of Engineering at Stanford University, can change the technological trajectory of a whole region. Fred Terman, considered the father of Silicon Valley, was the main instigator of two cornerstone endeavors that completely transformed the regions. First, he encouraged his former students to start their own businesses, such as Hewlett-Packard and Fairchild Semiconductor Corporation, in which he also played the role of an angel investor (Gibbons, 2000). As a result, Stanford's Electric Engineering department became a magnet for students who wanted to later launch their startups. Second, he launched Stanford Research Park in Menlo Park to accommodate startups. Following this initiative, MIT built the MIT Technology Square in the early 1960s as an incubator of high technology startups (Miller & Coté, 1987). In evolutionary economics, the dynamism of an economic system rests upon the absorption of scientific and technological knowledge, the diffusion of innovations within the innovation system, and the generation of scientific and technological knowledge (Iammarino, 2005).

The concept of path-dependency suggests that evolutionary patterns do not automatically lead to optimal outcomes. Paul David (1985) and Brian Arthur (1988) have contributed to the definition of the concept of path-dependency. The concept of path-dependency refers to the non-linear, self-reinforcing, historical economic processes that shape technological innovations. David argues that path-dependency in technological change has three determinants, namely, technical interrelatedness, economies of scale, and quasi-irreversibility. As shown by David with the QWERTY keyboard, path-dependency and technological trajectories are frequently spurred by temporally isolated events, which were provoked by chance elements rather than systematic forces. Indeed, as shown by Gould (1987), the QWERTY keyboard is an archetypal example of path-dependency that locked a technology into a suboptimal outcome. The QWERTY keyboard is the continuation of the typewriter's keyboard, which was before that, the keyboard used to write Morse codes for the telegraph. Although the QWERTY keyboard is arguably significantly less efficient than other keyboards' configurations, it is still the dominant keyboard design due to the process of path-dependency.

Arthur (1988) introduces the concept of self-reinforcing mechanisms to demonstrate that small historical events shape the nature of technology. Technological trajectories—the paths by which innovations in a given field occur—that are being chosen are by no means optimal (Dosi, 1982). Indeed, the path-dependent nature and changing nature of learning processes may act as dynamic entry-barriers with respect to possibly more efficient alternative technologies (See Utterback 1994). When the technology reaches a certain tipping point on a trajectory where the dominant design is accepted, cumulative processes reinforce and perpetuate that choice, highly reducing the spectrum of possible outcomes and alternatives. Since technological change is cumulative and path-dependent, influenced by the prevailing technological paradigm and the evolution of technological trajectories, it can get "stuck" or "locked-in" within one technological trajectory, which would potentially lead to sub-optimal results. Regions to a larger extent than countries, are prone to "lock-in" (Grabher, 1993). There is a strong cumulative process taking place in regions. Indeed, when a threshold of firms in the region has been reached, the region becomes more attractive for new firms to locate there, even if these firms have other locational preferences. The cumulative nature of science and technology combined with evolutionary notions of path-dependency and economics notions of increasing returns to scale result in a strong cumulative and self-reinforcing evolution of the spatial system. Older regions, like Paris and London, that enjoy strong urbanization economies due to a highly diversified economic base, tend to possess the potential to develop new technologies again and again, and to keep up with new regions that base their fortune on new technologies (Boschma & Lambooy, 1999).

The evolutionary economic approach has influenced the innovation system approach that aims to investigate how the innovation process is shaped within a national or regional scale. The concept of the National

System of Innovation (NSI), which was introduced by Freeman (1995), Lundvall (1992) and Nelson (1993), can be traced back to Friedrich List's book, *The National System of Political Economy,* published in 1856. In his book, List argued in favor of policies, among which were the protection of infant industries and the creation of vocational schools, to accelerate the industrialization of Germany, and to overtake England as the first European economic powerhouse. Freeman (1987, p. 1) defines the national innovation system as "the network of institutions in the public and private sectors whose activities and interactions initiate, import, modify and diffuse new technologies." The central theme is that innovation systems are evolutionary, path-dependent, and cumulative in nature; they evolve in a largely unplanned manner. The concept of innovation systems encompasses the analysis of the determinants of and the actors participating in the innovation process, and hence the concept provides an enticing framework for governments and policymakers to experiment with policy analysis, research, and design to strengthen their innovation systems.

The concept of a regional innovation system (RIS) provides a robust analytical and descriptive approach to understanding how the innovation process is shaped within a specific region (Asheim & Gertler, 2004). Doloreux (2003) defines a RIS as "a set of interacting private and public interests, formal institutions and other organizations that function according to organizational and institutional arrangements and relationships conducive to the generation, use and dissemination of knowledge." RISs mostly consist of two actors that interact with one another. The first and most important actors are the firms located in the region. The second actors are the regional institutional infrastructures that support the firms in the region, such as research and higher education institutes, technology transfer agencies, vocational training organizations, business associations, finance institutions. Interactions are central in RIS. Innovation systems are based on evolutionary, non-equilibrium theories in which innovation is a result of interactive processes both internal and external to the firm. In RIS, innovation is fully endogenous and constitutes an important determinant of economic change. Innovation processes involve evolutionary economic change, which is not linear and certain. In comparison to traditional economic analysis, innovation system models never reach an optimal equilibrium. Indeed, RIS has adopted conceptual elements of evolutionary economics and the new regional science, such as agglomeration, trust building, reciprocity, social network relationship, willingness to cooperate, institutions, and learning in regional systems.

CHAPTER 4

The Role of the Regional Government in the Innovation Process.

In the academic literature, there are different rationales for policy interventions. Regional innovation policies are increasingly subject to "policy-mix" recommendations to reduce market failures, system failures, and/or evolutionary failures (Flanagan, Uyarra, & Laranja, 2011). For neoclassical economists, government interventions distort markets, and, as a result, decrease social surplus and impose a deadweight loss upon society (Bator, 1958). Neoclassical economists acknowledge, however, that governments should intervene if and only if there is a market failure (that is, in a situation in which the free market is not producing an efficient level of allocation). There are four major types of market failures in which government intervention is frequent, the lack of public goods, which are non-excludable and non-rival goods; the existence of natural monopolies; negative and positive externalities, also known as spillovers; and informational asymmetries.

Regional policymakers are, however, increasingly designing regional innovation policies to reduce system and evolutionary failures due to the limitations of neoclassical economics to provide targeted regional innovation policy recommendations (see OECD, 2011a). The RIS approach emphasizes that regional governments can intervene to promote collective learning and to limit the dysfunctional interactions that lead to "system failures", as interactions between many different actors that cooperate, collaborate, and learn with each other, are central to the process of innovation (Laranja, Uyarra, & Flanagan, 2008; Smith, 2000). For some authors, system failures, rather than market failures, should be the starting point for policy intervention (Metcalfe, 2005). For Woolthuis, Lankhuizen, and Gilsing (2005), system failures include infrastructural failures (communication, energy, and science & technology infrastructure), institutional failures (hard failures when they refer to technical standards and legal system, and soft failures when they relate to norms and values), interaction failures (weak network failure when it is connected to a lack of complementary relationships, and strong network failure when it is linked to wrong direction network guidance), and capabilities failure (lack of competences). In EEG, regional innovation policies have to stir evolutionary mechanisms to promote variations and avoid lock-ins (Lambooy & Boschma, 2001).

In the innovation system approach, the process of regional lock-in has been extensively studied. The process of lock-in occurs due to the path-dependent nature of regional economic development and the cumulative nature of specific regional capabilities, which combine human, physical, and institutional endowments that lock regions into superior or inferior technological trajectories (Maskell & Malmberg, 1999a). Friedrichs (1993) for instance, shows that lock-ins can develop when local elites, such as corporate management, trade unions, and urban/regional managers or politicians, act to prevent structural changes in declining industries to protect their vested interests. The local elites tend, as a result, to prolong the period of crisis instead of proactively developing or attracting new types of economic activities. Lock-ins are most common in mono-industrial milieux dominated by large firms, for instance in the Ruhr region or Detroit (Maskell & Malmberg, 1999a). Grabher (1993) provides a framework to analyze lock-ins. He identified three types of lock-ins. First, functional lock-ins, which refer to rigid hierarchical inter-firm networks, particularly between large enterprises and small and medium-sized suppliers that can reduce the need for suppliers to develop boundary spanning functions, such as research and development and marketing. Second, cognitive lock-ins, which refer to the homogenization of worldviews or mindset. Third, political lock-ins, which relate to strong intertwined relations between public and private actors that might hinder necessary industrial restructuring.

The role of the government to stimulate technological innovations can also generate suboptimal outcomes and lead to government failures. Indeed, there are also many rationales against government intervention to foster technological innovations. Government failures arise due to the context-specific, complex, and dispersed nature of knowledge. Moreover, lobbies and vested interests can influence government decisions into sub-optimal policy choices. Because governments are extremely vulnerable to loss of reputation and are under continuous public scrutiny, policy responses to market and system failures take time to formulate due to bureaucratic processes and administrative oversights (Nooteboom & Stam, 2008). The academic literature reviews a large number of government failures, such as regulatory capture, that result from increased government intervention (Dal Bó, 2006). Regulatory capture, one of the most studied government failures, is "the process through which special interests affect state intervention in any of its forms". Regulatory capture for public regulators can take two forms. First, the revolving door phenomenon refers to the situation where a public regulator without electoral ambitions who might want to pursue a career in the private sector favors specific industries or companies in anticipation of future employment. Second, a public regulator might be constrained by political and reelection motives or personal self-interest derived from his or her position rather than wider public interests (Levine & Forrence, 1990). The theory of regulatory capture suggests that public or private entities can funnel direct and indirect subsidies distributed through public intervention. At the local and regional level, government intervention can take many forms: taxes, zoning regulations, public procurements, or policies for innovation. Any of these previously mentioned interventions can be shaped to favor a monopoly, public officials, or a set of private companies, and thus distort public interest. In a narrower sense, regulatory capture refers to the influence of state monopolies on governmental agencies to introduce regulations that benefit them.

Regulations also affect the quality of entrepreneurship. As shown by Baumol (1996), there are two types of entrepreneurs: the productive entrepreneurs who create value and the unproductive ones who extract profits from the system. The type of payoffs and regulations will affect the relative size of both types of entrepreneurs. Public policies to offset market or system failures can have a negative effect, such as crowding out, when private firms reduce their funding with public funds. In some instances, government funding may be a cheaper source of finance than funding raised from capital markets (Lach, 2002). As shown by Lerner (2009, p. 84), regulatory capture can affect government initiatives for the promotion of entrepreneurship, as with the case of the Australian Building on Information Technology Strengths (BITS), an incubator launched in 1999, whose funding went mainly to compensate the managers and not the incubated firms; other examples included NYC Discovery Fund and Iowa Heartland Seed Capital Fund.

Djankov, La Porta, Lopez-de-Silanes, and Shleifer (2002) show that entry regulations—procedures, official time, and official costs—for startups in more democratic governments are lighter than in less democratic ones, suggesting that stricter entry regulations favor politicians and bureaucrats. As a result, in order to maximize public interest, a diverse range of stakeholders from the public and private sectors as well as the civil society should ponder whether the reduced system and market failures is more beneficial than an increased likelihood of government failures. The potential failures that exist in innovation systems do not always make government intervention necessary or desirable. Indeed, while governments may improve overall welfare, they do not always have the willingness, capacity, or resources to do so (Dixit, 1996). Moreover, a policy failure, which is the failure for a policy to achieve its objectives, may arise due to the inadequate policy design, implementation, and governance.

The idea that the state should step back from the economy to unleash the power of entrepreneurship and innovation in the private sector has become pervasive to the extent that it is virtually accepted by the public as a "common sense" truth. The neoclassical dogma of the self-regulating free market is, according to Karl Polanyi (1957), a myth. Indeed, for Polanyi, there never was a truly free and self-regulating market system.

He said: "the road to the free market was opened and kept open by an enormous increase in continuous, centrally organized and controlled interventionism" (p. 144). Governments have always taken an active role in not only protecting their industries but also in stimulating new technologies (Mazzucato, 2015). Governments should go beyond their roles of creating the best business environment conditions for innovation to directly intervene in the economy.

Governments are frequently intervening to support public research. Government procurements, namely done in the defense sector, and government contracts give a strong incentive to private firms to conduct basic research. Public research undertaken by universities and public research institutions often are long-term, uncertain, and high-risk research that couldn't have been conducted by the private sector (Freeman & Soete, 2004). The invention of computers, for instance, was financed with government funding. The University of Pennsylvania received financial support from the Department of Defense in order to build the Electronic Numerical Integrator And Computer (ENIAC), the first electronic computer, whose main purpose was to calculate trajectories of shells and bombs (Freeman & Soete, 2004). The Bayh-Dole Act encouraged the emergence of the biotechnology industry since the new biotech companies were new spin-offs from university labs with heavy state funding (Mazzucato, 2015). Block and Keller (2016) found that between 1971 and 2006, the large majority of innovations have taken advantage of Federal research supports, especially in the early stage of development.

In the United States, the government has been proactive in establishing policies for the development of new technologies, such as the Defense Advanced Research Projects Agency (DARPA), the Small Business Innovation Research (SBIR), the Orphan Drug Act, and the National Nanotechnology Initiative (Mazzucato, 2015). The Pentagon created DARPA in 1958 as a response to counter the Soviet technological breakthrough and advances in launching the satellite Sputnik in 1957 (Mazzucato, 2015). The Federal Department of Defense introduced the concept of "blue sky thinking" in R&D projects to promote forward thinking inventions that could only potentially produce results in 10 or 20 years. The Reagan Administration built upon the success of DARPA in launching the Small Business Innovation Development Act (Mazzucato, 2015). The SBIR program required government agencies with large research budgets to designate a fraction of their research funding to support initiatives of small, independent, for-profit innovative firms, and startups. The major technological elements in Apple's iPhone can be traced back to state investments, from the Internet, to the touch-screen display, to the voice-activated SIRI personal assistant. As shown by Ghosh and Nanda (2010), while venture capital firms invest capital at the stage of the idea vetting and pre-commercial testing, governments and universities invest in basic and applied research. Private venture capital and private equity companies invest in companies whose commercial viability is established within a 3-to-5-year period (Ghosh & Nanda, 2010). In biotechnology, nanotechnology, and ICT, venture capital companies started to invest in companies 15 to 20 years after the most important investments were made by public sector funds.

Metropolitan-regions are increasingly seen as the most appropriate entities for designing supportive policies for science, technology, and innovation compared to nation states, which in an increasingly borderless world, are increasingly seen as dysfunctional (Ohmae, 1995). Additionally, from a policy perspective, it is more relevant to look at innovation strategies at the urban and regional scales than at the national scale since: regional innovation systems follow varied development paths; divergences in growth are sometimes more pronounced within countries than between countries; R&D and patenting are mostly concentrated in key regions in top OECD innovative countries; new regions are emerging as knowledge hubs; regional collaboration and networks are becoming increasingly relevant for innovation; and creative industries are strongly shaped by regional features (OECD, 2011a).

Regional innovation policies have evolved considerably in the past decades to respond to the unique conditions of the knowledge economy (Knight, 1995). Regional innovation policies have often tended to be shaped by "best practice models," such as "growing the next Silicon Valley," derived from well performing regions, which are then applied indiscriminately to regions around the globe (Sturgeon, 2000). Innovation policies must take into account specific system failures that can exist in their regions. Indeed, there is no "one-size-fits-all" regional innovation policy, as regions have different institutional contexts, prior innovation capabilities, and knowledge and industrial bases (Tödtling & Trippl, 2005). The main policy recommendation is to design place-based and place-sensitive policies to respond to regional innovation specificities (Barca, McCann, & Rodríguez-Pose, 2012). A place-based policy is "a long-term strategy aimed at tackling persistent underutilization of potential and reducing persistent social exclusion in specific places through external interventions and multilevel governance" (Barca, 2009, p. VII).

Regional governments have taken a more active role in shaping innovation policies due to the ongoing process of decentralization. The range and nature of competences devolved from central governments to regional governments will affect how regional innovation policies are designed. Countries, such as Belgium, Canada, Germany, Spain, and the United States have granted many competences for science, technology, and innovation (STI) policy to regions. At the other end of the spectrum, regions in small or centralized countries, such as Greece, New Zealand, and Portugal do not have many competences in designing STI policies (OECD, 2011b). Some regions, such as Baden-Wurttemberg or Rhône-Alpes have pushed for greater autonomy to develop their regional innovation policies.

Generic regional innovation instruments include but are not limited to: clusters and excellence hubs, incubators, science and technology parks, scholarships for post-graduate studies, public subsidies to private R&D, tax credits for private R&D, competitive research grants, promotion of scientific cooperation, funding via public development banks, public venture capital funds and guarantees, systemic initiatives in the form of networks, clusters, competitiveness poles and competence centers, innovation support services for existing SMEs, support for innovative start-ups, innovation vouchers, mobility and talent attraction schemes, support for quality research infrastructure, innovation procurement schemes fiscal measures, technology extension services, and technology platforms (OECD, 2011a). Regional innovation policies have to be flexible and to constantly evolve to avoid: autarkic frameworks, which emerge due to lack of openness to outside sources of knowledge and ideas, lock-in with respect to decision-making, which refers to incapacity to change technological trajectories, ineffective multi-level governance, which refers to coordination problems between different levels of governance, and innovation paradox due to limited institutional capacity (OECD, 2011a).

In 2000, the European Union made innovation a priority with the Lisbon Agenda and Europe Horizon 2020 strategy, which sets a target for 3% of the EU's GDP to be invested in R&D in 2020, along with a diverse range of innovation policies to close its technological gap with the United States and thus become "the most competitive and dynamic knowledge-based economy in the world capable of sustainable economic growth with more and better jobs and greater social cohesion" (European Parliament, 2000). The Horizon 2020 strategy has, however, not brought the desired innovation outcomes with R&D spending as percentage of GDP remaining flat since 2009. In 2015, R&D spending as percentage of the GDP has reached 2.01% in the EU-28 countries, compared to 3.29% in Japan and 2.79% in the United States. R&D intensity in China has even surpassed that of the EU-28 countries, with Chinese R&D expenditures reaching 2.07% of GDP in 2015 (European Commission, 2018b). While the United States has not promoted convergence among regions, the European Union with the EU Cohesion Policy has actively pursued convergence initiatives, dedicating €351.8 billion for the programming period 2014-2020. At the center of the EU Cohesion Policy are different regional innovation strategies, such as the Smart Specialization Strategy (S3), which is based on place-based strategy to prioritize activities related to existing regional capabilities (Foray, David, & Hall, 2009). Regions must design their Smart Specialization Strategy (S3) to be granted European Regional Development Funds (ERDF). The share of the EU Cohesion Policy dedicated to promoting regional innovation has grown from 4% for the programming period 1989-1993 to more than 50% for the new programming period 2020-2027 (European Commission, 2018a)

The different rationales for policy interventions and the "policy-mix" recommendations to reduce market failures, system failures, and/or evolutionary failures through place-based innovation policies under a multi-level governance setting imply that regional policymakers are dealing with extreme levels of policy complexity (Flanagan, Uyarra, & Laranja, 2011). Academics often have too much faith in the capacities of policymakers to design, coordinate, and implement innovation policy recommendations, and in the capacities of the regional innovation systems to break path-dependent evolutionary mechanisms (Flanagan & Uyarra, 2016). Regions are highly unequal when designing and implementing place-based policies. Influenced by the new public management (NPM), metropolitan and regional governments are establishing regional innovation agencies (RIA) as organizations within a wider institutional framework to strengthen regional innovation capacities. NPM is associated with doctrines of public accountability and organizational best practices with high levels of managerial autonomy, particularly regarding personnel and financial management (Verhoest, Van Thiel, Bouckaert, & Laegreid, 2012). Although managerial autonomy and reduced political influence might increase efficiency, effectiveness, and accountability, it adds a layer of policy complexity for regional governments in an already complex policy realm (Pollitt, Talbot, Caulfield, & Smullen, 2004). An RIA is an innovation intermediary that can be defined as "an organization or body that acts as an agent or broker in any aspect of the innovation process between two or more parties" (Howells, 2006, p. 720). There is a great diversity among them in terms of size, mission, activities, and ownership and funding structure (OECD, 2011a).

CHAPTER 5

The Entrepreneurial Region.

The concept of *The Entrepreneurial Region* applies the concept of *The Entrepreneurial State* at the regional scale. Fundamentally, the entrepreneurial region stresses that regional governments can play a fundamental role in promoting the innovation process and regional structural change. Conceptually, the entrepreneurial region complements the entrepreneurial state by providing a response to two shortcomings of the entrepreneurial state, namely its conceptual relevance for countries in the Global South and for regional governments. The entrepreneurial state is fundamentally concerned with promoting the next wave of disruptive innovations, which can only take place in a few countries with the critical threshold of knowledge base, institutional support, and financial resources, such as the twenty largest economies (G20) in the world, to foster knowledge recombination leading to disruptive technological innovations. It is hard to imagine how Uruguay, Mali, or Cambodia could compete with China or the United States in creating the next technological wave of artificial intelligence, self-driving cars, or robotization.

The entrepreneurial region provides a tool, the regional innovation agency (RIA), for lagging regions to catch-up technologically with leading innovative regions. There is a limited policy interest to apply the concept of the entrepreneurial region to innovation hubs in the knowledge core, such as Boston, New York, San Francisco, Paris, London, Shenzhen, Tokyo, as those regions already have strong path-dependent evolutionary mechanisms that have locked their industrial development into superior technological trajectories. The concept of the entrepreneurial region is really about regions on the knowledge periphery, regions remote from some of the main sources and users of knowledge, which have limited extra-regional knowledge linkages, knowledge infrastructures, and a limited capacity to absorb extra-regional knowledge. Roughly speaking, regions on the knowledge periphery are regions outside the Top-100 cluster by patent filing in the world and with limited knowledge flows coming from those regions.

Regions in the knowledge periphery suffer from multiple limitations that lock their industrial development into inferior technological trajectories due to the nature of scientific and technological knowledge. Indeed, regions on the knowledge periphery have a lack of endowments in scientific and technological knowledge, a low regional absorptive capacity, and an inertia in their socio-institutional structures. This lack of innovation capabilities is also constrained by a low quality of government and low institutional capabilities. The entrepreneurial region is ambitious since it aims to address all of the limitations facing regions on the knowledge periphery to catch-up technologically with regions in the knowledge core.

One of the instruments of the entrepreneurial region is the regional innovation agency (RIA). A RIA is an organization that is characterized by its autonomy from political influence, its wide mandate, and its managerial autonomy, particularly regarding personnel and financial. Basically, the entrepreneurial region aims to reduce these structural weaknesses by acting as knowledge gatekeepers to improve regional absorptive capacity, by increasing the amount of extra-regional scientific and technological knowledge to complement local knowledge capabilities, and by promoting radical socio-institutional changes to further increase regional absorptive capacity and extra-regional knowledge flows that will allow the region to catch-up.

The entrepreneurial region emphasizes the fundamental role of extra-regional scientific and technological knowledge for promoting regional structural change in regions located on the knowledge periphery. The acquisition of extra-regional scientific and technological knowledge is motivated by the search for capabilities, which firms in a peripheral innovation system might lack, and of the need to form alliances through which to build entirely new competences, and discovering new knowledge and innovations (Belussi & Sedita, 2010). In the innovation process, diffusion—and more importantly the speed of diffusion—matters more for economic development than innovation or invention (Ray, 1980). International technology diffusion determines productivity and growth differences, partly because only a handful of innovative metropolitan-regions account for most of the world's creation of new technology (Keller, 2004). During the industrial revolution for instance, Britain was highly successful in exploiting inventions produced in Continental Europe (Mokyr, 1990). Indeed, not only the acquisition and development of knowledge through innovation and learning but also the diffusion and efficient exploitation of this knowledge are relevant for economic growth (Narula, 2004).

The role of extra-regional scientific and technological knowledge has been critical in the rapid economic development of Japan during the Meiji restoration (1869), the Four Asian Tigers, and China (Amsden, 1989; Mokyr, 1990; Rodrik, 2008; Wade, 1990). In Japan for instance, during the Meiji restoration (1869), between 1872 and 1892, the government invited more than 5000 foreign experts to help run the government-owned factories and to provide training to Japanese workers (Dahlman & Nelson, 1995). The industrial revolution in Europe benefited from inventions made in China or in the Middle East. Leibniz implored the Jesuit traveling to China "not to worry so much about getting things European to the Chinese, but rather about getting remarkable Chinese inventions to us; otherwise little profit will be derived from the Chinese mission" (as cited in Mokyr, 1990, p. 188). Regions on the knowledge periphery, however, lack the capacity to acquire, absorb, and exploit scientific and technological knowledge from regions located in the knowledge core. In sum, extra-regional knowledge can reduce the risk of technological, institutional, and organizational lock-ins and promote technological innovations through recombination with local knowledge.

Empirical studies confirm the importance of external knowledge in the innovation process. In a study of the biotechnology cluster in the Boston area, Owen-Smith and Powell (2004) emphasize the importance of global knowledge pipelines, which refer to communication and collaboration between local firms and research centers with inter-regional and international partners, for accessing new knowledge. Owen-Smith and Powell find that local buzz and international networks contributed to the success of the cluster. The inter-organizational networks at the local level and through proprietary alliances were critical to generate externalities and enhance the innovative capacity of the firms located in the biotechnology cluster in Boston. Rantisi (2002) studies the openness of the Garment district in New York City and shows how intermediary institutions facilitate the transmission of ideas between the Lower East Side of Manhattan and the Garment district.

The entrepreneurial region underlines the importance of regional absorptive capacity for supporting new technological trajectories, also referred to as new industrial path development in regions located on the knowledge periphery. The acquisition and diffusion of extra-regional scientific and technological knowledge must be coupled with policies that aim to strengthen regional absorptive capacity in order to support regional actors in fully exploiting the extra-regional knowledge. At the firm level, the successful exploitation of external knowledge requires the creation within firms of absorptive capacity, which is the capacity to understand externally sourced technology and apply it internally (Cohen & Levinthal, 1990).

Wesley Cohen and Daniel Levinthal (1990) define the concept of absorptive capacity as "the ability of a firm to recognize the value of new, external information, assimilate it and apply it to commercial ends" (p. 128). The concept of absorptive capacity emphasizes the importance of external knowledge and of the needed internal capacities to translate that external knowledge. Cohen and Levinthal (1989, p. 569) suggest that R&D not only generates "new information but also enhances the firm's ability to assimilate and exploit existing information." The importance of intra-firm absorptive capacity is exemplified by the quote of Lew Platt, former chairman of Hewlett-Packard, when he stated, "if only HP knew what HP knows, we could be three times more productive!" (as cited in Gertler, 2003, p. 84).

The agents that facilitate a firm's absorptive capacity are called knowledge gatekeepers. At the level of a firm, the exchanges of knowledge go through a two-step process, in which certain key individuals act as bridges linking the organization members to the outside world (Allen, 1977). The knowledge gatekeepers work as a medium between the creator of information and its users. The two-step process between the creator and the users of information is frequent in social sciences. For instance, Lazarsfeld, Berelson, and Gaudet (1944) found, in a study of voter decisions during the 1940 presidential election campaign, that information from radio and newspaper did not influence the average voter directly, but rather through "opinion leaders" who subsequently influenced the vote of friends and associates.

The knowledge gatekeepers are thus able to operate within and transmit between two coding schemes and have a dual role: the acquisition of external knowledge and its translation. According to Allen (1977), knowledge gatekeepers are "a small number of key people to whom others frequently turned for information. These key people differed from their colleagues in the degree to which they exposed themselves to sources of technological information outside their organization" (p. 145). In RISs, knowledge gatekeepers play an important role in determining absorptive capacity and favoring collective learning process.

The entrepreneurial region must support radical socio-institutional changes, for two reasons. First, the entrepreneurial region has to align the socio-institutional structure with the new industrial path development to support the RIS' absorptive capacity to fully exploit extra-regional knowledge. Second, the entrepreneurial region has to limit transitional failure resulting from structural change in the economy. Structural change in the regional economy implies rapid path creation and path destruction that affects the socio-institutional structure, which, in turn, through cumulative causation will affect future path development. As pointed out by Carlota Perez (2010), during structural change in the economy, such as during a Kondratieff cycle or during the introduction of disruptive innovations, the socio-institutional structure is briefly decoupled from the techno-economic structure due to its relative inertia and path-dependent nature compared to a period characterized by rapid increasing technological complexity and by the diffusion of technological disruptions. The Information and Communication Technology (ICT) revolution for instance, has completely transformed the innovation system to the point of triggering major structural adjustments, such as the changing desired skills in the labor force, the emergence of new management structures and types of organizations, the emergence of new industrial relations, and the emergence of institutional regulation structures at the national and international level (Castells, 1996).

The socio-institutional structure refers to the evolutionary structures that co-evolve with the techno-economic structure. The socio-institutional structure involves three knowledge-driven structures: (i) the social structure that refers to informal institutions, (ii) the organizational structure that refers to organizational features within private organizations, and (iii) the institutional structure that refers to the organizations that implement and/or devise formal institutions. First, the social structure refers to informal institutions, i.e "the conventions and codes of behavior" (North, 1990, p. 4). More precisely, informal institutions are common law, customs, traditions, taboos, codes of conduct, work norms, norms of cooperation, conventions, practices, and so on (Edquist & Johnson, 1997). One of the main issues concerning this type of enabler is that strong internal social structures such as technological conservatism, tradition, custom, and routine can produce economic inertia and conformism and, as a result, can be powerful obstacles to innovation and technological change (Mokyr, 1990).

For Headrik (1988), the cultural diffusion of technology takes "a willingness to accept changes, a strong political cohesiveness, and a common vision of the future" (p. 13). Informal institutions also affect incentives and behaviors as in the case of entrepreneurship due to attitudes related to risk-taking, failure, status, and prestige (Edquist & Johnson, 1997). Second, the organizational structure refers to organizational features through "the implementation of a new organizational method in the firm's business practices, workplace organization or external relations" that favors technological innovations (OECD, 2005, p. 51). Third, the institutional structure consists of the public organizations that directly implement or devise formal institutions, such as the regional and local governments, universities, high schools, linkages organizations, or research centres. Formal institutions are the "rules that humans devise", such as laws, constitutions, government regulations, formal instructions, and property rights, that affect transaction costs (North, 1990, p. 4). Intellectual property rights, for instance, such as laws and rules concerning patents, copyrights, and trademarks affect the level of appropriability of technological innovation and thus the diffusion of knowledge (Edquist & Johnson, 1997). Institutions are "enabling or constraining mechanisms" that affect the level of knowledge transfer and interactive learning (Boschma, 2005).

In summary, the entrepreneurial region aims to address regional structural weaknesses that are specific to regions on the knowledge periphery. One of the instruments of the entrepreneurial region is the regional innovation agency (RIA) that can be defined as an executive agency that designs and implements place-based policies to respond to those regional structural weaknesses. Regional innovation agencies have five important characteristics. First, the private and the public sectors must have a shared vision for the RIA. Second, the right level of governance for the RIA is the metropolitan region, as the RIA's coordination of multi-level governance will lead to institutional complexity and coordination failures. Third, the RIA must mobilize the most important actors in the RIS coming from the private sector, the public sector, academia, and the civil society. RIAs are seen as more legitimate in mobilizing a diverse range of actors than are regional governments, which might be politically motivated. Fourth, the role of the RIA is to monitor its RIS and successful RISs around the world, to identify weaknesses in its RIS, to locate the actors with the capacities to address those weaknesses, and design and support the implementation of the place-based programs to generate these capacities in their RIS. Fifth, the RIA must coordinate multiple quadruple helices at numerous decision levels from the definition of the strategic priorities and the identification of weaknesses, to the design, implementation, and evaluation of the place-based policies. The five implications are specific to regional innovation agencies and are conditional upon good governance and key principles being prescribed in new public management, such as autonomy and public accountability. We will see in the next chapters, the specific case of Medellín's innovation agency, Ruta N.

Part II

The Story of Medellín's Economic
Transformation

CHAPTER 6

The Country Context – Colombia.

Map 1. Map of Latin America and Colombia. Source: own design.

Introduction. Colombia is a country in South America, a continent that has experienced periods of economic volatilities and political instabilities. South America's instabilities are the outcome of the region's heavy reliance on extraction and exportation of its raw materials resulting from the institutional legacies established by former colonizing countries, namely Spain and Portugal (Bértola & Ocampo, 2012). For the last two centuries, the continent's GDP per capita has fluctuated around the world average. Colombia's capital city is Bogotá. The country has a total area of 1,141,748 km^2 and shares borders with Brazil, Ecuador, Panama, Peru, and Venezuela. The country has a rich biodiversity with a territory that contains the Amazon rainforest, the Andes mountain range, and the

Caribbean and Pacific Coastlines. Colombia is the second most populous country in South America with 49,834,240 inhabitants, behind Brazil's, 207,652,865 inhabitants, but ahead of of Argentina's, 43,847,340 inhabitants (DANE, 2018). The three largest cities are, Bogotá with 7,878,783, Medellín with 2,464,322, and Cali with 2,369,821 inhabitants (DANE, 2018). As of 2016, Colombia has the third largest GDP in South America, current GDP of USD $282 billion or USD $5,805 per capita. Brazil, has a current GDP of USD $1,796 billion or USD $8,649 per capita, and Argentina, current GDP of USD $545 billion or USD $12,440 per capita (World Bank, 2018).

The Construction of the Nation State (1810-1903). After Colombia's independence from the Spanish Empire on July 20, 1810, to the end of the 19th century, Colombia underwent a period of construction of its nation-state. The construction of the nation-state was marked by confrontations between two political parties, the Liberal and the Conservatives, and between two visions for the nascent Colombian nation, centralism versus federalism. During the construction period of the nation-state, Colombia's economic development was stagnant. Indeed, from 1800 to 1905, the GDP grew at an average rate of only 1.7% per year, a rate comparable to the population growth (Kalmanovitz & López, 2006). Moreover, the internal market was not integrated. Colombia consisted of small, local markets that were geographically separated and isolated due to its topographic idiosyncrasy.

In the mid-19th century, the liberal government initiated bold socio-economic reforms. The most important reforms were the expulsion of the Jesuits, the separation of the Church and the state, the introduction of the civil marriages and divorce, the privatization of education, and the abolition of slavery (Caballero Argáez, 2016). The 1853 Constitution promulgated two fundamental liberal reforms: universal suffrage granted to all adult males and the introduction of the federal political and administrative system. The federal Constitution of Rionegro adopted in 1863 renamed Colombia, the United States of Colombia. The conservative party violently opposed the reforms and Constitutions introduced by the liberal party. In the 1860s and all the way through the 1880s, social unrest and conflict between the liberal and conservative parties was rife. The state, due to its federal nature, was weak in dealing with the political and social unrest. As a result, the 1886 Constitution was adopted to end the period of instability by profoundly reinforcing the centralized nature of the Colombian state (Piedrahita Echeverri, 1988). The 1886 Constitution reintroduced the role of the Catholic Church as the main regulator of social life, the strong role of the president who could directly appoint and dismiss mayors and governors, and revoked liberal reforms. The Colombian Constitution of 1886 led to a concentration of power that resulted in an inefficient and rigid state with limited political legitimacy (Ramírez Moreno, 2006).

The confrontation between the two parties culminated in the Thousand Days War (1899-1902) after the conservative political party had imposed their Constitution in 1886 (Arias Trujillo, 2011). The inability of the central state to negotiate with the United States for the concession of the Panama Canal led to the separation of Panama in 1903. At the end of the Thousand Days War, President Reyes (1904-1909) introduced a range of industrial policies, such as an increase in tariffs for final goods and government subsidies to initiate the process of industrialization and to end political unrests. The industrialization was made possible due to coffee exportation that rapidly expanded in the 1880s. Indeed, the coffee exportation allowed the "diversification of the economy" and to support "nascent industrial development" (Arias Trujillo, 2011, p. 15).

The State in Conflict (1903-1991). In the 20th century, the Colombian economy went through three shocks that favored the emergence of three economic periods: the loss of Panama in 1903 after the Thousand Days War; the great depression in 1929-1932; the economic opening in 1989-1991 as a consequence of globalization and the collapse of the USSR. Colombia's economic development was concurrent with one of the most violent civil wars in the history of the world, *La Violencia*, which mutated into Colombian internal conflict.

The acceleration of Colombia's industrialization was caused by: the expansion of the coffee production and exportation between 1905 and 1929, which resulted in the formation of an internal market for manufactured goods; the creation in the beginning of the 20th century of light manufacturing companies, and the adoption of protectionist macroeconomic policies. Coffee exports experienced a rapid growth between 1905 and 1930. Indeed, coffee production multiplied by six, from 500,000 to 3,000,000 bags a year; and during the same period, Colombia's GDP multiplied by three (Caballero Argáez, 2016). The industrial dynamics depended much on the foreign currency exchange reserve, and as a result, on coffee exports, which represented up to 80 percent of the total Colombian exports in the 1950s. From 1930 to 1990, international coffee prices determined the internal business cycles of the Colombian economy, both in its long-run economic development and in its short-term economic development due to the volatility of coffee prices. Coffee was the engine of internal demand and foreign currency exchange reserve. During the Great Depression (1929-1932), the national government adopted highly protectionist trade barriers and tariffs as well as a series of public work projects to overcome the economic crisis, which created the conditions for the consolidation of the coffee and industrial sectors.

World War I, World War II and the Great Depression demonstrated the limitations of the agro-export model and the importance for Colombia to develop a strong industrial sector. In Latin America, the export sector was limited to raw materials, and in the case of Colombia, to coffee exports. Indeed, between and 1940 and 1970, coffee represented more than 70% of all Colombian exports (Restrepo Santamaria, 2011). In the 1950s, the national government adopted import-substitution and protectionist policies as a national development strategy, which coincided with the peak in power of the industrial elite. Industrial production proliferated between 1945 and 1955. In the 1950s, the share of the industrial sector in the economy was higher in Colombia than in any other Latin American country. The import-substitution model, which was pushed by the United Nations Economic Commission for Latin America and the Caribbean (ECLAC), ultimately created, however, an uncompetitive industrial export sector.

The industrial and coffee sectors have largely determined Colombian economic policies implemented between 1930 to 1990. The macroeconomic policies were greatly influenced by two associations: the National Federation of Coffee Growers (FedeCafé) founded in Medellín in 1927 and the National Association of Industrialists (ANDI) founded in Medellín in 1944. The ANDI was created in response to the suggestion of President Alfonso Lopez Pumarejo (1942-1946) who proposed to only have one industrial representative from Antioquia to consult with the national government (Caballero Argáez, 2016). The macroeconomic policies promoted by the ANDI and FedeCafé did not only favor the industrial and coffee sectors but also contributed to the delay in the development of other economic sectors.

In 1930, after 50 years of conservative governments, the Liberal Party managed to return to power, partly due to internal disagreements within the Conservative Party. The Liberal Party remained in power from 1930 to 1946 (Arias Trujillo, 2011). In 1946, the Conservative Party won back the Presidency and tensions between Liberals and Conservative reemerged. The tensions took a dramatic turn with the assassination of the liberal party presidential candidate Jorge Eliécer Gaitán in 1948, which officially marked the beginning of *La Violencia*. The period of *La Violencia* was extremely complex in that it involved many different actors who had widely diverse motivations. Indeed, *La Violencia* involved a class conflict, religious persecutions, criminal organizations, state violence, and a conflict between Liberals and Conservatives (Arias Trujillo, 2011).

In 1953, General Gustavo Rojas Pinilla staged a military coup to put an end to *La Violencia*, which led the Liberal and Conservative parties to enter into an agreement in 1958, known as *El Frente Nacional*, to alternate in the political office. The political elites from the Liberal or Conservative parties were able through *El Frente Nacional* to retain the political power for themselves, a tactic frequently used between elite groups in Colombia to protect themselves from external threats. *El Frente Nacional,* however, did not end the violence. Indeed, the agreement was the catalyst for the creation of left-insurrectionary militias, such as the *Ejército de Liberación Nacional* (ELN) and the *Fuerzas Armadas Revolucionarias de Colombia—Ejército del Pueblo* (FARC–EP) in 1964. The internal conflict reemerged through new actors. First, came the left-insurrectionary guerrillas in the 1960s, then, the narco-traffickers in the late 1970s, and finally, the paramilitaries in the late 1980s.

The internal conflict was fueled with drug money that deeply penetrated all layers of Colombian society, from politicians and farmers to guerrilla fighters and bankers. In order to deal with the extreme level of violence and internal conflict, the state had to formulate a "new social contract" in which the paramilitaries were supported by the most authoritarian actors within the state (Arias Trujillo, 2011). Political and economic elites, particularly landowners and agro-industrialists, tacitly supported the creation of self-defense groups to stop left-wing guerrilla groups from extorting local businesses. From 1958 to 2012, the Colombian conflict claimed the lives of at least 220,000 people, 81.5 % of whom were civilians (Grupo de Memoria Histórica, 2016). Since 1958, around 5 million people have been internally-displaced (Grupo de Memoria Histórica, 2016). The peak of violence was reached during 1988 and 1989 when Pablo Escobar and other narco-traffickers pressured the state to end the extradition treaty between Colombia and the United States (Arias Trujillo, 2011). During the 1990 presidential campaign, three candidates were assassinated (Caballero Argáez, 2016).

The internal conflict and the Latin American debt crisis in the 1980s forced the political elites to adopt political and economic structural reforms. As for many other Latin American countries, the economic reforms that Colombia introduced in the 1980s were pushed by multilateral development banks, namely the International Monetary Fund (IMF), as a prior condition of applying for international credit loans. The reforms ended protectionism, redefined the role of the state, introduced flexible labor laws, and eliminated state monopolies (Restrepo Santamaria, 2011). In addition to economic reforms, the state started to discuss political and social reforms. The internal conflict challenged the legitimacy of the state. President Belisario Betancur (1982-1986) was the first President to recognize that the left-insurrectionary guerrillas had legitimate causes, such as fighting for social justice and against political exclusion (Arias Trujillo, 2011). Betancur's (1982-1986) peace process initiative included negotiation, social reforms, and opening up the political space (Arias Trujillo, 2011). In 1988, mayors were for the first time elected through universal suffrage and not appointed through presidential decree. The political reforms initiated in the 1980s paved the way to the introduction of a new Constitution.

The Modern State (1991-present). In the 1990s, Colombia engaged in structural institutional and economic reforms, which led to the creation of modern Colombia. In the late 1980s and early 1990s, President Virgilio Barco Vargas (1986-1990) and President César Gaviria Trujillo (1990-1994) initiated the process of "Colombia's economic opening." The economic reforms included reforms in international trades, foreign direct investment, taxation, labor, and privatization, that were greatly influenced by "Washington Consensus" economic policies. In 1991, tariffs were decreased from 50% to 15% and many non-tariff barriers were eliminated (Restrepo Santamaria, 2011). The economic reforms were opposed by the industrial and agricultural sectors but welcomed in the financial and service sectors (Franco Restrepo, 2006). On July 4, 1991, President César Gaviria Trujillo (1990-1994) signed the new Constitution that replaced the political Constitution of 1886 and became the symbol of "Colombia's economic opening." The 1991 Constitution is a democratic milestone that redistributed power between the executive and the judiciary, guaranteed social rights to minority groups, limited traditional power structures, decentralized some economic and fiscal authorities to regions and municipalities, and encouraged participatory democracy and social inclusion (Palacios, 2006). The 1991 Constitution led the guerrillas to reassess the legitimacy of their armed struggle. Additionally, the 1991 constitution promoted administrative decentralization with the creation of four territorial entities: departments, districts, municipalities, and indigenous territories. The Constitution also introduced two instruments of municipal strategic planning, namely, the Municipal Development Plan in 1994 and Territorial Organizational Planning in 1997.

The Colombian Constitution of 1991 deferred to regions some authority to design and to implement Science, Technology, and Innovation (STI) policies (Sánchez Mejía, 2011). Law 29 of 1990 in Science and Technology promotes the organization of a Science and Technology Strategic National System led by the National Council and the Technical Secretariat Colciencias. In the 1990s, Colciencias recognized the importance of regions in participating and in coordinating the National System of Science and Technology. In 2011, the General System of Royalties was created through the Legislative Act 05 amending articles 360 and 361 of the Constitution. The General System of Royalties is a mechanism to redistribute the state revenues from the exploitation of non-renewable resources to finance strategic projects in STI in Colombia. 10% of the General System of Royalties are distributed between the Colombian regions to finance projects in Science, Technology, and Innovation (STI) at the regional level through the Science, Technology and Innovation Fund (STIF). The purpose of the fund is to strengthen the region's capacities in STI as well as to contribute to social and economic equity between regions and to regional competitiveness.

In the 1990s, the government of Colombia engaged in controversial methods to end the internal conflict. In 1993, Decree 2535 authorized civilians to use military weapons. In 1994, Decree 356 authorized the creation of legal paramilitary structures, the *Servicios Especiales de Vigilancia y Seguriadad Privada*, also known as CONVIVIR, to maintain control over guerrillas' activity zones (Amnesty International, 2005). The controversial government of Alvaro Uribe (2002-2010) had a mandate to restore security in the country and to defeat the guerrilla groups. *Plan Colombia,* a United States foreign aid, military, and diplomatic program, allowed the Colombian state to have near unlimited resources to fight left-insurrectionary guerrillas (Arias Trujillo, 2011). For Uribe's supporters, who constitute a large majority of Colombians, Uribe has allowed Colombia to enter an era of peace, competitiveness, and confidence. On November 2016, the government of Juan Manuel Santos (2010-2018) signed a peace deal with the *FARC-EP* paving the way to the end of the Colombian internal conflict.

CHAPTER 7

The City Context – Medellín.

Medellín – Introduction. The dazzling landscapes of Medellín and its heavenly climate have stirred the admiration of many foreign travelers. In 1825, the French geologist and mineralogist Juan Bautista visited Medellín and reported in his writings that "if Paris did not exist, I would decide to live in Medellín" (as cited in Ortiz Mesa, 1996, p. 289). The city of Medellín was founded in 1616 after the Spanish conquerors led by Jorge Robledo discovered the Aburrá Valley on August 23, 1541 (Alvarez, 1996, p 57). The people from the region of Antioquia are commonly known as *Paisa*, who are proud of their distinct culture, especially from the capital city Bogotá.

The city of Medellín is located in the Aburrá Valley in the midst of the Andes mountain range. The valley is approximately 7 kilometers wide and 30 kilometers long with a total area of 1,157 km^2 (Hermelin, 1996). At the center of the valley is the Medellín River, which receives its water from a multitude of streams. The urban center is at an altitude ranging from 1,400 to 1,800 meters above sea level surrounded by mountains that peak above 3,000 meters above sea level. The altitude at which the urban center lies and its closeness to the Earth's equator create unique climatic conditions. The climate is stable all year long with daily temperatures ranging from 18 to 26 degrees Celsius and average annual precipitation of 1,500 mm. The city of Medellín is the capital and the largest urban center in the department of Antioquia. In 2015, the population was 2,464,322 in Medellín and 3,777,009 in the Aburrá Valley (City of Medellín, 2018). The city of Medellín is part of the Aburrá Valley Metropolitan Area, including the cities of Itaguï, La Sabaneta, La Estrella, Caldas, Bello, Copacabana, Girardota, Barbosa, Medellín, and Envigado. The city of Medellín is divided into 16 comunas; they are: Popular, Santa Cruz, Manrique, Aranjuez, Castilla, 12 de Octobre, Robledo, Villa

Hermosa, Buenos Aires, La Candelaria, Laureles-Estadio, Las Américas, San Javier, El Poblado, Guayabal, and Belén.

The Mining City (1826-1904). During the Spanish colonial period (1616-1810), Medellín was a small town that had no political or economic importance. In the first census conducted in Medellín on October 19, 1675, there were 221 families, ethnically distributed as followed: 45% mixed race (black and white); 23% mestizo (American Indian and white); 18% white; 13% American Indians (Alvarez, 1996, p. 57). In the 18th century, immigrants to Antioquia and to Medellín were mostly composed of Andalusian, Basque, and Extramaduran. The discovery and exploration of gold in the region and its designation as the capital of the province of Antioquia in 1826 provoked the city's economic development.

Mining was the main economic activity in the region until the end of the 19th century. Gold production doubled between 1750 and 1779 and then quadrupled between 1780 and 1880 (González Escobar, 2007, p. 14). The mining boom was accompanied by a thriving agricultural economy, namely sugar cane, coffee, and cocoa, and growing internal demand for manufacturing goods. The expansion of the agricultural and mining sectors led the mining and political elites to invest in large infrastructure projects, such as the railroad (1874-1914), the telegraph (1867), and bridges over the Cauca river in Jerico (1881) and Santa Fe de Antioquia (1895) to connect Medellín with international trade routes (Molina Londoño, 1996). Between 1820 and 1880, the mining sector favored the emergence of a business elite and commercial activities, first with Jamaica and then with Europe. In 1870, Charles Saffray, a French Botanist, reported that in Medellín "there was no export trade since the city only had gold, which was sent abroad to import large quantities of merchandises, such as irons and cotton from England; hardware, toys, and matches from Germany; fabrics from Switzerland; footwear, clothes, hats from Spain; and medicines from France" (as cited in Caballero Argáez, 2016, p. 59). By 1870, Medellín was the second largest city in the country with 29,795 inhabitants, after Bogotá with 40,883 inhabitants (Alvarez, 1996).

The mining elite realized that an increase in mining productivity, and thus profitability, could be achieved by the introduction of technological innovations from abroad (González Escobar, 2007, p. 32). In the 1820s, engineers like Carlos Segismundo de Greiff or Tyrrel Moore and technicians like Enrique Hauesler and Julian Jones came to Medellín to work in the mining sector. In his book, *Immigrant Engineers and Scientists in Colombia 1760-1950*, Poveda Ramos (2011) shows the importance of foreign engineers, most notably from England, Germany, Sweden, and France, in diffusing knowledge, especially in the mining sector, in Colombia, namely in Medellín. Poveda Ramos (2011, p. 255) points out that almost all important innovations in the mining sector in Colombia, except for the Antioquia mill, were brought or invented by foreign engineers. In 1898, another French explorer Pierre d'Espagnat stated: "Medellín is the center of the gold region, it is where mining businesses, gold ingots, and mining reports converge" (as cited in Alvarez, 1996, p. 77).

From 1880, coffee exploitation and production became the main economic activity of the Antioquia economy, since the region of Antioquia has not only the best climate to produce coffee but also high-quality volcanic soils (Restrepo Santamaria, 2011). Coffee and mining were the two most important determinants of Medellín's industrialization. Indeed, coffee and mining were the connection between agriculture and industry that allowed Medellín to branch into new industrial activities. The expansion of coffee production generated a strong internal demand for agricultural machinery and for intermediary goods. Moreover, the mining and agricultural sectors fostered the development of workshops and steel and iron foundries that would later pave the way for the process of industrialization.

This rapid economic development had critical cultural repercussions on the inhabitants of Medellín who were, as pointed out by José Manuel Restrepo, culturally backward and spent their time engaging in "disputes to know whether Medellín was better than Rionegro" (as cited in González Escobar, 2007, p. 16). At the end of the 19th century, Januario

Henao Álvarez, Antioquia Secretary of the Treasury and the first Secretary of the Chamber of Commerce of Medellín, pointed out the importance of developing a local industry to limit the city's reliance on imports (Molina Londoño, 1996, p. 221). Antioquia's economy went through a deep structural crisis that reached bottom in 1904 with the bankruptcy of the public sector (Molina Londoño, 1996, p. 212). The crisis was a determining factor for the political and business elites to initiate the process of Medellín's industrialization.

The Industrial City (1904-1981). In Medellín, the process of industrialization underwent four stages. In the first stage (1904-1929), the protectionist policies that were put in place in 1904, the rapid growth in coffee exports, the entrepreneurial economic elites with their Calvinist ethos, and the accumulated industrial knowledge related to mining, allowed Medellín to develop a light manufacturing and durable consumer industry, such as textile, soft drinks, beers, cigarettes, and household appliances (Valencia Restrepo, 1996). In 1904, the soft drinks company Posada Tobon, Postobón, was founded. In 1905, Medellín hosted the first industrial exhibition in Colombia. In 1907, the textile company Coltejer was founded. The engine of industrialization was coffee exportation, which created a robust internal demand for industrial machinery and allowed economic surplus to be reinvested in supporting the infant industries, and by 1920, Medellín was the most important industrial city in Colombia (Caballero Argáez, 2016).

In the second stage (1929-1945), the industrial diversification was motivated by the shortages of imported essential goods from Europe and the United States during the World Wars (Valencia Restrepo, 1996). Industrial growth was also stimulated by large government projects that were undertaken during the Great Depression (1929-1932). In 1932, the national government undertook the construction of large infrastructure projects, such as the Oyala Herrera Airport in Medellín, and the hydroelectric dam in Guadalupe (Poveda Ramos, 1996).

In the third stage (1945-1973), Medellín was an industrial powerhouse. The industrial sector greatly benefited from import-substitution and protectionist policies effected after World War II. The economy grew between 1945 and 1956 at an average annual growth rate of 11% (Valencia Restrepo, 1996, p. 483). In 1967, Daniel Herrero, who investigated Medellín's industrial development between 1925 and 1965 pointed out that "Medellín is the Latin American's Manchester. The city has often been compared to São Paulo. The textile activity has constituted the driving force of the industrial development in the city" (as cited in Valencia Restrepo, 1996, p. 476). In the 1950s, Medellín was producing up to 90 % of Colombian textiles and ranked first in Latin America in terms of uses of textile machinery.

Life Magazine (1947) depicted Medellín in an article as a "capitalist paradise," where people are "devoutly Catholic." The industrialist families, such as the Restrepos and the Echeverrías, shaped a paternalistic working-class ethos. For instance, the workers at the textile company Coltejer, "like thousands of others in the city, are docile, well-trained well cared for. The company offers bonuses, paid vacations, cheap housing, stock-investment plans, while at the same time paying high dividends and expanding plant facilities" (Life Magazine, 1947, p. 116). The textile factories offered to the working class "a respectable occupation under the patriarchal protection of family firms and the Catholic Church" (Hylton, 2007, p. 74). Medellín was relatively unaffected at the beginning of *La Violencia,* and benefited from it through displaced refugees to work in the growing industrial sector. The ANDI and the industrialist families painted the image of a city being "a peaceful oasis of capitalist productivity" thanks to the benevolence of its industrial elites (Hylton, 2007, p. 76). Medellín, however, attracted many displaced people from the internal conflict and economic migrants in search of work and of a better life in the industries. The fast-growing population in the 1960s and 1970s led to the creation and expansion of informal settlements, to which the local authorities responded with repression and evictions (Hylton, 2007).

In the fourth stage (1973-1981), the industrial sector went through a deep structural crisis. In the late 1970s and early 1980s, the industrial sector in Medellín was confronted with the worst crisis in its history. The crisis was caused by both external and internal factors. The external factors can be summed as: the recession in developed countries after the 1973 and the 1979 oil crisis; the decreased coffee prices on international markets; and the increased competition from the Four Asian Tiger Economies in the textile, automobile, and industrial sectors. The internal factors can be summed as: the lower industrial sales; low investments in industrial capacities; the low investments from the government in infrastructures, namely transportation infrastructures; national macroeconomic policies, such as the protectionist policies; smuggling due to protectionist policies; and the trade union's operations to sabotage or slow down production (Valencia Restrepo, 1996). The city was confronted at the same time to waves of internally displaced refugees and economic migrants looking for jobs in the industries. One of the main consequences of the industrial crisis was the inability of the city to absorb additional workers and the subsequent rise in unemployment and expansion of informal settlements. Indeed, the city of Medellín has grown during its industrial stage at an exponential rate from 100,000 inhabitants in 1925 to 1,100,000 inhabitants in 1975 (Restrepo Uribe, 1981).

The Narco City (1981-2003). Medellín became a narco city due to: the inability of the industries to absorb the workforce fleeing Colombian's internal conflict in the 1970s, the concentration and spatial distribution of poverty in some neighborhoods, the strategic position of the city in the cocaine production and distribution routes, and its smuggling knowledge (Maclean, 2014). From the narco city would emerge a complex and violent conflict involving non-state armed actors, such as the narco-traffickers, left-insurrectionary militias, criminal gangs, and paramilitary, and state actors. The informal settlements on the hillside of the city were the recruiting ground and the battleground of the conflicts between the different non-state armed actors. The narco-economy quickly expanded since it provided unheard-of job opportunities and upward social mobility for the youth without prospects of education or waged work (Hylton,

2007). The social and cultural transformation in the 1970s that accompanied the transformation of Medellín into a narco-city were important. Indeed, Medellín was "the most conservative city in the most conservative country" in Latin America (Hylton, 2007, p. 71). The narco-city redefined the social and cultural contexts of Medellín. The narco elites from narco-trafficking with their "glitzy tastes and violence" were in dramatic contrast with the "piety and conservatism" of the industrial elite (Hylton, 2007, p. 78).

In the 1970s, Medellín was an important smuggling center—namely cigarettes and alcohol—from the duty-free zone of Panama to dodge the high import tariffs resulting from protectionist policies. Before becoming the Medellín Cartel kingpin, Pablo Escobar was fighting the Marlboro wars with rival criminal gangs to acquire the monopoly over contraband cigarettes. In 1981, Pablo Escobar formed the death squad, *Muerte a Secuestradores* (death to kidnappers), which would later be known as the Medellín Cartel. Pablo Escobar, who once called himself Robin Hood, funded social programs, built soccer fields, churches, and even an entire neighborhood for Medellín's poorest inhabitants, receiving, as a result, their sympathies (Lamb, 2010). At its peak in the late 1980s, the Medellín Cartel controlled 60 percent of the Colombian cocaine traffic and employed up to 120,000 people, including 2,000 to 3,000 persons in the United States (Filippone, 1994).

The downfall of Pablo Escobar began when he was elected as deputy and forced to resign from the Chamber of Representatives in 1982 (Hylton, 2007). The catalyst to stop Escobar, came, however, with the assassination of the presidential candidate Luis Carlos Galán in 1989 (Hylton, 2007). The Colombian government backed the Drug Enforcement Agency (DEA) demand for Escobar's extradition, which he responded to with a campaign of bombings and targeted assassinations of pro-extraditionists, such as journalists, university professors, and judges as well as directly confronting the state with the assassination of 500 policemen between 1990 and 1991 (Hylton, 2007, p. 82). The search block, *Bloque de Búsqueda,* and the DEA finally killed Pablo Escobar on December 2, 1993.

In parallel to the narco-economy, left-insurrectionary militias and paramilitary groups emerged. The left-insurrectionary militias were formed to take control of failed-neighborhoods controlled by criminal gangs. The FARC took control of *Comuna* 13, the M-19 of the Eastern *Comunas,* and the ELN of the Northeastern *Comunas.* The left-insurrectionary militias legitimized the use of violence due to the high rates of poverty and exclusion in Medellín. These actors replaced the state in the failed-communities providing security and social services while at the same time reproducing the authoritarian methods that they fought against in the first place. With the expansion of the left-insurrectionary militias and the Medellín Cartel, right-wing paramilitaries and vigilant groups emerged. Diego Fernando Murillo Bejarano, also known as Don Berna, led the *Bloque Cacique Nutibara* (BCN), an important paramilitary organization in Medellín. Don Berna was a leading figure in the *Perseguidos por Pablo Escobar* (PEPES), a death squad to kill Pablo Escobar, and *La Oficina de Envigado*, a drug cartel and criminal organization that took over the activities of the Medellín Cartel (Amnesty International, 2005).

In the early 1990s, right-wing groups, such as *Amor por Medellín* or *Mano Negra*, were undertaking social cleansing to eliminate "undesirables", such as petty criminals, drug addicts, communists, and prostitutes from Medellín's streets (Restrepo, 1992). The left-insurrectionary militias were the highest enemies of the Colombian state, in front of the drug-cartels and the paramilitaries, leading the most authoritarian elements of the Colombian state to tacitly support the paramilitaries (Hylton, 2007). The conflict between and within non-state armed actors and the state in Medellín led to a period of extreme violence. In 1991, at the peak of violence, there were 381 homicides for 100,000 inhabitants in Medellín, that is almost 40 times higher than what the United Nations (UN) consider epidemic violence.

The industrial and political elites had a responsibility in the emergence of violence in the city due to their inability to create inclusive growth during the industrial period of prosperity (Maclean, 2014). In the late 1990s, 0.3 percent of the Colombian population controlled 60 percent of the productive land, 10 percent of the population held 58 percent of national income; and unemployment reached 20 percent (Avilés, 2006, p. 391). The political and business class also contributed to the violence through their clientelism and complicity with non-state armed actors, namely right-wing paramilitary groups (Maclean, 2014). From the 1970s to 2000s, Franco Restrepo (2006) argues that there was a rupture between the political and economic elites in Medellín and Antioquia. The rupture caused an absence of political and territorial projects binding the elites together to promote regional development. The causes of this rupture are diverse, among them, the reorganization of regional industrial activities, the context of violence, the emergence of the "narco-elite", and the changing political and power structures.

In 1988, the Mayor of Medellín was, for the first time, elected through universal suffrage. Indeed, from 1948 to 1987, there were 49 different Mayors directly appointed by presidential decree, averaging an office tenure of 10 months, which greatly hindered any long-term, or even short-term, planning (Alcaldía de Medellín & Banco Interamericano de Desarrollo, 2009). The local government began to adopt transformative social, economic, and institutional policies. The program PRIMED started in 1993 as a pilot project between the City of Medellín, the governments of Colombia and Germany, and the United Nations Development Program (UNDP) to improve the quality of life of the residents in some of the poorest neighborhoods of the city through urban upgrading (Echeverri & Orsini, 2010). The *Empresa de Desarrollo Urbano* (EDU) was created in 1993 by the city to plan urban development and Territorial Organizational Plans. In 1995, the Medellín Metro, which is the only train-based public transit system in Colombia, was inaugurated. After a visit to the Guggenheim Museum in Spain, Mayor Luis Pérez (2001-

2003) decided to build the first cable car line in Medellín to create "something emblematic" for Medellín (Martin, 2012).

In the years 1998-2002, Medellín endured its worst economic crisis since the great depression (Restrepo Santamaria, 2011). The effects of the crisis were strongly experienced in Antioquia and Medellín, which suffered not only a deep economic recession but also a social crisis as well. In 2001, the city had an unemployment rate of 22% and a homicide rate of 169 for 100,000 inhabitants (Gómez, Aparicio, & Urbano, 2015). The economic crisis was seen by different elites, as either an opportunity or as a threat. The new elites who were involved in finance, real-estate, and service wanted more integration of the city into the world economy, while the old industrial elites wanted to engage in more protectionist measures.

The decline in violence in Medellín is due to multiple factors, such as: local policies, namely the transportation and infrastructure projects that addressed exclusion; investments in the poorest areas of the city; the creation of public spaces and parks; investment in education; attention to solidarity and competitiveness; and increased participation and community involvement in policy. National policies, global trends, and informal institutional changes have also contributed to the decline in violence in Medellín, such as the Colombian Constitution of 1991, the election of mayors, globalization, closer ties with the USA, and the end of the cold war, the style of leadership, cultural capital, the increased participation, and the reduced corruption (Maclean, 2014).

In summary, the global trends, informal institutional changes, national and local policies all contributed to the "Medellín Miracle," which refers to the rapid decline in violence experienced in the city since 1993. Some authors point out, however, that the decline in violence was achieved through the monopoly over illegal activities of one non-state armed actor, namely Don Berna with *La Oficina de Envigado*, leading to a tacit agreement between the local authorities and the drug lord (Amnesty International, 2005). Indeed, following Pablo Escobar's death in 1993 and the military operations—operation *Mariscal*, operation *Orión*, and *Estrella VI*—conducted by the state to reclaim the *comunas* controlled by the left-insurrectionary militias in 2002 and 2003, Don Berna established total control over the city and homicide rates started to fall precipitously. In June 2003, the BCN issued a communiqué in which they stated their responsibility in the rapid fall of homicides in Medellín contributing to the necessary climate for attracting foreign direct investments to Medellín (Amnesty International, 2005)

Towards the Knowledge City (2004-present). For many academics, politicians, and journalists, Medellín has since the early 2000s transformed itself into an "urban miracle". For *The Guardian,* Medellín has transformed "from murder capital to model city" (Brodzinsky, 2014). For the *New York Times,* "Medellín's Nonconformist Mayor Turns Blight to Beauty" (Romero, 2007). From 1991 to 2016, Medellín's homicide rate has been divided by fifteen and, is thus safer than many cities in the United States, like Detroit (Michigan), New Orleans (Louisiana), or Chicago (Illinois).

The "Medellín's miracle" has, however, some grey areas. In 2006, President Uribe extradited 13 paramilitary commanders, including Don Berna, which resulted in a spike in the homicide rate in Medellín during the years 2007, 2008, and 2009 demonstrating the violation of the tacit agreement between narco-traffickers and the local authorities (Martin, 2012). Criminal gangs have occasionally captured participatory budgeting to consolidate power in their controlled territories (Caracol Radio Medellín, 2017). The city had in 2015, and still has, a very high GINI coefficient of 0.49 and is still a very unequal city with HDI ranging in 2012 from 98.67 in Poblado to 80.88 in Popular (City of Medellín, 2018). Moreover, "narco-elite," also known as *"clase emergente,"* still pose a threat to the economic and social transformation of the city (Franz, 2018).

	2002	2009	2015	Percentage Change (2002-2015)
Population in Medellin	2 129 874	2 317 336	2 464 322	15,7
Unemployment Rate	16,7	15,7	9,0	-45,9
Poverty Rate	36,1	23,9	14,3	-60,4
GINI Index	0,55	0,53	0,49	-10,9
Homicide Rate per 100 000 inhabitants	177	94	20	-88,7

Table 1. Medellín's Selected Key Indicators from 2002 to 2015. Source: City of Medellín (2018), DANE GEIH (2018).

The group of actors at the center of the transformation of Medellín into a knowledge city is the *Grupo Empresarial Antioqueño* (GEA), an informal network of the largest companies and *multilatinas* in Medellín. The reorganization of the GEA strategic priorities, the threat from "narco-elite" to the GEA, and the elections of Mayor Sergio Fajardo (2004-2007), Alonso Salazar (2008-2011), and Aníbal Gaviria (2012-2015), which were backed by the GEA, have led to structural reforms in education, social urbanism, social inclusion, and innovation-led policies; have paved the way to Medellín's economic transformation to more knowledge-based activities. Indeed, the realignment of interests between the business elites and the political class during the mandates of Sergio Fajardo (2004-2007), Alonso Salazar (2008-2011), and Aníbal Gaviria (2012-2015) was unprecedented since the 1970s.

Mayor Sergio Fajardo Valderrama (2004-2007), the poster child of the "Medellín's miracle", was invited to participate in the politics of the city at the initiative of Proantioaquia (Fajardo & Andrews, 2014). The political party led by Fajardo was the *Compromiso Ciudadano*, a broad coalition that emerged as a civic movement in the 1990s, involving public actors, the "reflexive middle-class", academics, nongovernmental organizations, the media, and the local business elite (Franz, 2017). The civic movement became a political party that was able to break the Liberal versus Conservative hegemony. Despite his inexperience, Sergio Fajardo (2004-2007) managed to bridge the private and the public sectors into participating in common regional projects thanks to his contacts with Proantioquia and the GEA. The limited capabilities of Fajardo's cabinet were compensated for his close links with the private sector. The symbol of his mandate, the Spanish Library, that is located in one of the poorest *comuna* has received a large administrative support from COMFAMA, which is influenced by the GEA. Fajardo's administration prioritized education to combat income inequality and violence, under the umbrella programs, "Medellín, the most educated", as the engine for social transformation (Alcaldía de Medellín, 2007).

The decline in violence is associated with the approach to urban development pioneered in the city known as social urbanism. Social urbanism is an umbrella term for the policies enacted in Medellín in the late 1990s and the early 2000s to address some issues facing the city's poorest neighborhoods. The comprehensive strategy of Social Urbanism was inspired by urban best-practices, namely in Rio de Janeiro and Barcelona, and national experiments, namely in Bogotá and the *Programa Integral de Mejoramiento de Barrios Subnormales de Medellín* (PRIMED) in Medellín in 1993 (Echeverri & Orsini, 2010). Social urbanism includes diverse strategic elements to promote spatial inclusion through urban projects, such as action zones, Integral Urban Projects to intervene in informal settlements, the linking of strategic processes, the transparent city, public spaces, mediation spaces, and leadership (Alcaldía de Medellín, 2012). The social policies were supported by the elites who understood their role in the crisis that affected the city and the historical debts owed to the poorest areas of the city. The programs that have been implemented can, however, be seen as an extension of the elite power into social and cultural aspects of the city.

The neoliberal reforms that have accompanied the internationalization of the Colombian economy resonated in Medellín with local policies and programs to promote entrepreneurship and innovation such as *Cultura E, Medellín Mi Empresa, Medellínnovation, Medellín Digital, Ciudad E, Medellín Ciudad Clúster, Medellín Ciudad para la Vida, CREAME, Parque E, Ruta N* and the *CEDEZOs*, among which Ruta N is by far the most ambitious program that has been implemented. In Medellín, the first policy programs to promote entrepreneurship were introduced in the early 2000s with the program *Medellín Emprende* and *Red Unificada de Emprendimiento de Antioquia* (RUEDA). Many programs undertaken by the municipality were made possible thanks to the resources that EPM-UNE transfers to the municipality, which allow investments in infrastructures, including the metro, metro cable, libraries, and parks; in entrepreneurship programs, and in education (Maclean, 2014). In Latin America, the low tax rates at the local level translate into under-capacitated and passive local governments. In Medellín, the low fiscal revenues are largely compensated for by the mandatory 30% transfer of EPM net annual profits to the municipal budget (Bateman, Durán, & Maclean, 2011).

Medellín has greatly integrated itself in the global economy. Foreign Direct Investment (FDI) increased by tenfold between 2002 and 2009 and Medellín became one of the top Latin American cities for doing business (Moncoda, 2016). In the past two decades, due to the reorganization of the GEA and of the city's economic structure, the city is increasingly moving towards more knowledge-based and service-based activities. Employment in the manufacturing sector has relatively declined from 2001 to 2017 by 29.42% while employment in service sectors, namely real-estate, construction, transportation, and commercial services has increased in relative terms. Although the share in its contribution to the economy has declined from 20.8% in 2003 to 18.1% in 2015, the manufacturing sector is still the largest sector in Medellín (City of Medellín, 2018).

In 2013, Medellín was awarded the Innovative City of the Year by the Wall Street Journal and Citibank (WSJ, 2013). Upon accepting the award, Mayor Aníbal Gaviria (2012-2015) pointed out that Medellín is "constantly reinventing itself" (Moncada, 2016). The reinventions are made possible thanks to the commitment of the economic and political elites to engage in ambitious regional projects. The public organization at the center of the transformation of Medellín into a knowledge city is Ruta

N. As Mayor Aníbal Gaviria (2012-2015) pointed out, "an outstanding case of this model of development and transformation of the city is Ruta N" (Almirall et al., 2016, p. 144).

CHAPTER 8

The Actors in the Creation of Ruta N.

Ruta N's creation has been a collective process involving triple helix actors, namely public institutions, private companies, and universities. There are many actors that have participated in the creation and the formulation of Ruta N. Four actors, however, have played a fundamental role in the creation of Ruta N. They are: The City of Medellín, Proantioquia, the Center for Science and Technology of Antioquia (CTA), and the public-owned multi-utility and communications company EPM-UNE. In addition to those four actors, the University-Firm-State Committee (CUEE), EAFIT University, the Medellín Chamber of Commerce for Antioquia, and Ruta N's first director and employee, namely Andrés Montoya and Juan Pablo Ortega have played an important role in Ruta N's creation.

The City of Medellín. Mayor Sergio Fajardo (2004-2007) was fundamentally concerned with education. Indeed, Fajardo's administration strategy was dubbed, "Medellín, the most educated" (Fajardo Valderrama, 2007). In 2007, 40% of the city's annual budget went to education and ten schools were built under Fajardo's administration (Fajardo Valderrama, 2007). Mayor Alonso Salazar (2008-2011), building on Mayor Sergio Fajardo's legacy, prioritized during his mandate, innovation and inclusiveness. Mayor Alonso Salazar (2008-2011) presented in his Development Plan 2008-2011, *Medellín is Inclusive and Competitive,* in Chapter 3, Economic Development and Innovation, Section 3.1. Component: Creation and Support of Companies, Subsection 3.1.1. Program: Support for Entrepreneurship, 3.1.1.4. Project: The "Entrepreneurship Block" (*Manzana del Emprendimiento*). The Development Plan 2008-2011 defines the "Entrepreneurship Block" as "a physical space to consolidate science, technology, and innovation in the city" that should be led by EPM and the city's planning department

(Alcaldía de Medellín, 2008, p. 87). The project, the "Entrepreneurship Block," which would later become known as Ruta N, was instigated by the Municipality but was, however, ill-defined. Neither the Mayor nor his administration knew what the "Entrepreneurship Block" should be. Mayor Alonso Salazar wanted an organization that could support the development of regional high value-added and highly competitive technologies, such as in healthcare where Medellín has a strong competitive advantage.

> "When I was running for Mayor of Medellín in 2007, I was thinking that we needed a project to give a regional dimension to innovation, something with a wider reach. We looked at Chile that was successful in creating high value-added products. We wanted to do something similar with Ruta N" (personal communication, 17 August 2018).

> "In the plan of the Mayor, there was something called the 'Entrepreneurship Block', but no one knew what an entrepreneurship block was. It was supposed to be a physical space [...] but with our interdisciplinary group, we started to investigate what was happening in the world and what needed the city, from there, we concluded that the city, more than an entrepreneurship block, needed to focus its efforts on issues related to science, technology, and innovation" (personal communication, 17 July 2017).

Proantioquia. *Proantioquia* is a not-for-profit organization that was created on July 1975 as an initiative of the private sector. The entity's constitution was signed by 12 industrialists from Antioquia who were united to seek the progress and development of Antioquia through transformative projects. *Proantioquia* aims to mobilize the business sector to influence public policies to create favorable conditions for the development of the region, such as better human capital, business-friendly environment, and more inclusive development. In influencing public policies, *Proantioquia* carries out three roles: first, the role of a think-tank; second, the role of an incubator for strategic projects or institutions; and third, the role of an opinion leader.

Proantioquia is the unofficial not-for-profit organization of the *Grupo Empresarial Antioqueño* (GEA), which is an informal group of large regional companies that make up around 80% of Medellín's GDP and contributes up to about 8% of Colombia's GDP (Franz, 2018). In the late 1970s, notorious industrial companies in Medellín, such as *Coltejer*, *Postobón*, and *Cervunión*, were hostilely being taken over by industrialists from outside Antioquia, such as Ardila Lülle, Santo Domingo, and Sarmiento Angulo (Calle, 2015). In March 1978, a group of industrialists from Antioquia formed the *Sindicato Antioqueño,* later known as *Grupo Empresarial Antioqueño* (GEA), as an informal association that had for mission to defend each other interests, to not speculate, and to not accept foreign investors (Calle, 2015).

Once described in *Business Week* as "The Other Medellín Cartel", the GEA is a Keiretsu-like conglomerate where companies have cross-ownership, which has allowed them to reinvest their profits in long-term projects, to avoid hostile takeovers, and to be immune to the influence of narco-money (Restrepo Santamaria, 2011). The GEA was able, for instance, to prevent the hostile takeover of *Cementos Paz del Rio*, a GEA member, by *Cemex*, the Mexican cement company, by recapitalizing the company with the government the company (Lane, 1996). The industrial crisis in the late 1970s led the GEA to envision for the region an economy geared towards service-based and knowledge-based activities, such as financial services, real estate, tourism, and service (Calle, 2015). The GEA has a significant impact in the development of the city and the region to the extent that there is a belief that if Medellín is doing well, then the GEA will be doing well (Schipani, 2014). The GEA's three dominant companies are the investment banking and insurance company, *Grupo Sura*, the food processing company, *Grupo Nutresa*, and the cement company, *Grupo Argos*.

The emergence of a new elite structure since the 1980s that has developed close links with narco-traffickers and paramilitary groups has been challenging the established industrial elite, namely the GEA (Franz, 2018; Salazar, 1990). The industrial crisis combined with the increased rivalry from "narco-elite", also known as *clase emergente*", pushed the GEA to reorganized itself into becoming more globalized and integrated (Franz, 2018; The Economist, 2001). Indeed, the transition from the industrial to the service and innovation economy, the process of globalization, and the internationalization of capital implied a restructuration of the strategic industries towards the financial and service sectors (Franco Restrepo, 2006). Thanks to the GEA's high reinvestment rate due to its cross-ownership structure, the GEA began a process of expansion and internationalization of their activities with the creation of *Multilatinas*, mostly in Latin America, which affected their visions for the Medellín and Antioquia (Restrepo Santamaria, 2011).

In the late 1990s and 2000s, the GEA established strategic alliances with international companies, among them Noel-Danone (France), Noel-Bimbo (Mexico), Éxito-Casino (France), Corfinsura-International Finance Corporation (Washington, the United States), Argos-Holcim (Switzerland), Suramericana-Munich Re (Germany), to access the latest technologies, know-how, capital, and business knowledge, while most importantly retaining control of the companies (Londoño, 2004). In the past decades, the GEA has increasingly been involved in the political economy of Medellín to secure their vested interests and to counteract the influence of the "narco-elite" on the political class. The GEA has participated in the creation of many public-private partnerships with the municipal government and of many cultural and social projects in the city, such as Ruta N, the CUEE, the CTA, the ACI, Plaza Mayor, Museums, Tecnnova, which allow the GEA to put pressure on the municipal and regional governments to have transparent public management (Franz, 2018). Newly-elected Mayors or Governors, such as Luis Pérez Gutiérrez, Mayor of Medellín from 2001-2003 and Governor of Antioquia from 2016-2019, who represent the *"clase emergente"* elite and are against

GEA vested interests, will have, as a result, a more limited influence to conduct reforms (Franz, 2018). Indeed, Mayor Luis Pérez Gutiérrez (2001-2003) is considered by the GEA as the Mayor and Governor who has been the most opposed to their interests (Restrepo Santamaria, 2011).

Proantioquia and its president Rafael Aubad were the most important protagonists in modeling Ruta N. *Proantioquia* played the role of an institutional incubator, shaping Ruta N's governance model, vision, structure, and strategy, while providing conceptual, operational, and management supports. *Proantioquia* organized meetings between the business sector and Ruta N and helped the Ruta N team to validate the model to the Mayor's office. Moreover, before being officially incorporated, Ruta N's first office was located inside *Proantioquia*'s office. The primary motivation for *Proantioquia* to support Ruta N was the necessity for the region to upgrade its entrepreneurial capacity, to upgrade its innovation capabilities, and to generate new entrepreneurs and high-growth startups. For *Proantioquia*, Medellín has to become more integrated into the global economy and to move away from its industrial past to transform itself into a knowledge city.

> "For Ruta N, which was an initiative brought by the Municipality, we [Proantioquia] wanted to incubate the initiative to support it, to support in defining the governance model, to support in defining the strategic lines, and to support in structuring the project as an organization" (personal communication, 8 August 2017).

The *Empresas Públicas de Medellín* (EPM-UNE). The *Empresas Públicas de Medellín* (EPM) is the largest multi-utility company—water, energy, waste, and UNE telecommunications—in Colombia. EPM was created on August 6, 1955, under the Municipal Agreement 058 during the exceptional regime of Gustavo Rojas Pinella, as an autonomous, independent, decentralized entity from the municipality of Medellín resulting from the merger of different utility companies, including the *Sociedad de Mejoras Públicas* (SMP). The multi-utility company is 100%

owned by the municipality of Medellín and is the object of collective pride for the inhabitants of Medellín no matter their socio-economic background. EPM, which is one of the largest companies in Latin America, reinforces the sentiment of an inherent efficiency and distinctive public administration in Medellín. In the 2000s, EPM began a process of expansion and internationalization of its activities by investing in other Colombian cities, such Bogotá, Cali, and Bucaramanga, and in other Latin American countries, such as Chile, Panama, Ecuador, Guatemala, El Salvador, and in the Panama Canal (Dinero, 2009). In 2006, EPM created UNE telecommunications as a separate entity in partnership with the telecommunication company Millicom International Cellular (Luxembourg).

The public multi-utility company is closely intertwined with Medellín's political economy. Indeed, EPM is the consolidation of the *Sociedad de Mejoras Públicas* (SMP), which was created by the industrial elite to influence the political economy of the city (Botero Herrera, 1996; García Estrada, 1999). EPM is largely influenced by two elite groups, the politicians from the City of Medellín and the GEA. Mayors, highly-ranked public officials, and even the former President of Colombia, Alvaro Uribe Vélez, have previously worked for EPM. Mayor Sergio Naranjo Pérez (1995-1997) initiated the debate to transform EPM into a public-private company, which was met with resistance in Medellín, most notably in El Poblado, the most affluent neighborhood in the city (Franco Restrepo, 2006). The public multi-utility company is mandated to contribute 30% of its net annual profit to the city's budget, which has valued EPM to be portrayed as the "surprising company behind the transformation of Medellín" (Ashoka, 2014). Indeed, the company has collaborated with the municipality in constructing libraries, parks, schools, transportation infrastructures, Ruta N, and the *Agencia de Cooperación e Inversión en Medellín y Área Metropolitana* (ACI). In contrast with other cities in Colombia and Latin America, Medellín's poorest neighborhoods are well-endowed in public utility infrastructures, such as access to water and electricity, thanks to the work of EPM.

EPM together with its telecommunications subsidiary UNE were fundamental in the creation of Ruta N since they are the ones financing the project, to the extent that the Ruta N's project had to be first validated by Proantioquia and EPM-UNE before being approved by the Medellín's Municipal Council. Moreover, UNE along with the city of Medellín, the ACI, EAFIT University, and the National Government were successful in attracting Hewlett Packard (HP) into the Ruta N building complex thanks to tax-breaks and heavy diplomatic backing from the local and national governments (Semana, 2011). The arrival of HP made the creation of the third building in the Ruta N building complex financially viable. HP was supposed to operate the Global Support Center for Latin America in Medellín, to occupy a building of 15,000-square-meter, to employ up to 400 persons, and to invest around USD $100 million in the city (Nearshore America, 2015; Samper, 2012).

The *Centro de Ciencia y Tecnología de Antioquia (CTA)*. The Center for Science and Technology of Antioquia (CTA), a not-for-profit organization, was created by Proantioquia with the support from Colciencias and the Antioquia Region in 1989. The industrial and business elites at the time drafted a strategic plan, titled *Antioquia Siglo XXI*, in which science and technology were to become the basis of the economic transformation of the region during a period of the city and the region characterized by an extreme level of violence. The CTA was to coordinate the city's economic transformation through the articulation, generation, and transfer of scientific and technological knowledge. The CTA has 18 different partners, namely 7 universities, 3 public institutions, and 8 private companies and has been a leading actor drafting strategic development plans for Medellín and Antioquia and creating the *Parque Explora,* a science museum.

In the 2008-2011 Medellín Development Plan, the City of Medellín planted the idea of building a physical space for entrepreneurship. There was a risk, however, that the building would become a "white elephant" or "cathedral in the desert." As a consequence, the CTA promoted the idea that the hardware (infrastructures and urban amenities) had to be complemented with the software (skills and knowledge) and orgware (learning and capacity-building). The CTA was contracted to draft the conceptual and architectonic components. For the architectonic part, the CTA did a referencing of best practices around the world of physical spaces for entrepreneurs and startups, such as MaRS Innovation in Toronto, Monterrey in Mexico, Googleplex in Silicon Valley, and 22@ in Barcelona. The CTA contracted the architects who designed the building Ruta N, namely Alejandro Echeverri and Emerson Marín, who have been involved in well-known architectural projects in Medellín. For the conceptual part, the CTA provided a financial model, an organizational model, wrote the institutional bylaws, and drafted the programs and work areas.

The CTA designed Ruta N's financial and institutional model to limit the influence of the municipality on the organization. Indeed, the board of directors includes private companies, public institutions, and universities. The financial model aimed to make Ruta N financially independent through collecting the rents from the offices located in the Ruta N buildings. The independence of the organization, relative to the local and regional governments, is necessary in order for Ruta N not to fall victim to political rivalries between the political elites and the business elites. The CTA pointed out that Ruta N should become a center for innovation and business (*centro de innovación y negocios*). Moreover, the CTA envisioned the role of Ruta N as a "city manager" supporting the municipality to adopt best-practices related to science, technology, and innovation.

CHAPTER 9

The Ruta N's Model.

The definition of Ruta N's model involved many actors in addition to the actors previously mentioned. The definition of the model was the outcome of interviews and meetings with the private sector, public sector, universities, and the civil society; the participation of venture capital managers, such as Esteban Velasco, and entrepreneurs, such as Diego Ángel; of benchmarking international best-practices, such as 22@ Barcelona, Barcelona Activa, the Galicia region and Basque Country in Spain, Israel, Singapore, Silicon Valley, Toronto, MIT, and Startup Chile; and of the assessment of initiatives at the local level as well as the roles of Medellín's innovative actors in the regional innovation system.

> "At the beginning of Ruta N, we benchmarked some projects, we looked at MIT, we looked at Toronto, we looked a lot at Barcelona and its innovation district. What we did was referencing best-practices from around the world" (personal communication, 28 July 2017).

The definition of Ruta N's model was the outcome of the participatory process led by Proantioquia and the CTA involving the most important regional leaders coming from the private sector, public sector, universities, and the civil society. The benchmarking of best-practices and participation of experts led to the creation of specific Ruta N's programs. More importantly, Ruta N's model tried to respond to specific regional needs that the existing linkage organizations in the regional innovation system were not addressing. In 2008-2009, Medellín had several intermediary organizations promoting science, technology, innovation, and entrepreneurship. Ruta N, for that matter, had to be different from the existing intermediary organizations in the regional innovation system, such as the *Parque Explora, Tecnnova, Parque E, CREAME*, or the technology park of Antioquia. From the assessment, Ruta N was first conceived as an intermediary organization (*entidad de segundo piso*) focusing on strengthening the capacity in science, technology, and innovation of the existing STI actors in the regional innovation system.

"In the beginning, Ruta N was conceived as an intermediary institution working with actors of the system, the City of Medellín, CTA, Chamber of Commerce, CREAME, Parque E to strengthen them in order for them to operate the programs" (personal communication, 17 July 2017).

Mission, Vision, and Strategic Priorities. Ruta N's mission is to support Medellín's transformation from an industrial into a knowledge city. As pointed out by Federico Gutiérrez, Mayor of Medellín 2016-2019, "we were the industrial capital of Colombia in the 20th century, but due to new global dynamics, we reinvented our economic calling. Today, thanks to Ruta N, we are stimulating our innovation ecosystem, to move towards a knowledge economy" (Ruta N, 2018a, p. 4).

Ruta N's overarching vision is to position Medellín in 2021 as the most innovative city in Latin America. This vision has, however, been redefined to become, "innovation will be the main driver of the economy and the city's quality of life" with the mega that "1.21% of economic growth will be the result of innovation activities" (Ruta N, 2018a).

The Official Creation. The Corporation Ruta N Medellín (*Corporación Ruta N Medellín*) was officially incorporated on November 11, 2009. Ruta N's bylaws state that: "the corporation is a not-for-profit organization, which has for corporate purpose the guidance, participation, coordination, consolidation, organization, promotion, development, diffusion, and operation of the policy and activities related to science, technology, innovation, and technology-based entrepreneurship, in all the areas that are deemed relevant for its Associates, within the City of Medellín's economic development policy, including public-utility, such as energy, water, information and communication technologies, as well as its complementary and related activities, specific to one and everyone of them" (Ruta N, 2010a).

On August 21, 2010, the Medellín's Council approved the municipal agreement 49 of 2010, which officially binds the municipality of Medellín to the Corporation Ruta N Medellín (Gaceta Oficial N°3730, 2010). Article 2 of the municipal agreement 49 of 2010 confers COP $9,167,000,000 to Ruta N operations for the year 2010 (Gaceta Oficial N°3730, 2010, p. 8). Article 4 of the municipal agreement 49 of 2010 points out that the Corporation Ruta N Medellín will be the entity leading matters related to Science, Technology, and Innovation in the Municipality of Medellín (Gaceta Oficial N°3730, 2010, p. 8).

The Building Complex and its Location. Since the Fajardo's administration, social and/or economic transformation has to be embedded in urban transformations. Indeed, the Fajardo administration's prioritization of education led to the creation of hard infrastructures, such as libraries and schools. Medellín's knowledge turn, as a result, had to start with the creation of a building dedicated to Science, Technology, and Innovation.

The Ruta N building complex is located between Carabobo and Cundinamarca with the street Barranquilla in the northern part of the city for three reasons. First, the *Parque Explora*, which is located in the northern part of the city, had a reserved empty lot that could be used for construction. Second, the northern part of the city was selected due to its existing infrastructures, such as the University of Antioquia, the National University in Medellín, the *Hospital San Vicente de Paul*, the *Parque Explora*, the *Parque E*, the *Parque de los Deseos*, the Botanical Garden of Medellín, two metro stations—Hospital and Universidad—and its proximity to downtown Medellín. Third, the northern part of the city of Medellín has historically been an impoverished area, concentrating most of the city's poverty and violence. Indeed, the area was known to be the city's garbage dump. Ruta N participates in the City's New North strategy

(*Nuevo Norte de la Ciudad*), an urban regeneration strategy to transform the area into a business and innovation district.

Ruta N's Role in the Regional Innovation System. Ruta N's role is to support Medellín's transformation from an industrial city into a knowledge city with the objective to support new regional industrial path development and to promote structural change in the economy. The creation of a public institution dedicated to Science, Technology, and Innovation implies that the benefits should be greater than the costs it generates. In other words, the potential government failure generated from intervening in the market should be compensated for by limiting a wide range of failures produced by the market, namely market, system, and evolutionary failures. The rationale for government intervention was motivated by Medellín's relative isolation from global knowledge flows. From the 1970s to 2000s, Medellín was isolated from international knowledge flows due to a period of extreme violence, as well as due to idiosyncratic cultural, social, and geographical factors. This isolation contributed to the cognitive and political lock-ins of the industrial sector, which hindered the region's paths creation and paths branching into more knowledge-based activities. Regions on the knowledge periphery have limited access to extra-regional knowledge and absorptive capacity, which contribute to system failures and required, as in the case of Medellín, some sort of policy intervention. Ruta N was created out of a specific context. Indeed, Medellín has been relatively isolated from the global knowledge flows, which has been accentuated by specific geographical, social, and institutional barriers that limited the acquisition, absorption, and the diffusion of extra-regional knowledge into its RIS.

The city of Medellín is located in a mainland valley surrounded by majestic mountains. This specific geographic dimension has led the city to not only be relatively isolated from the rest of the world but also from the rest of Colombia leading to nurture the idiosyncratic "Paisa culture". In 2018, according to Google Maps, the city of Medellín is located by car some 7 hours and 44 minutes from Bogotá, 7 hours and 39 minutes from Cali, and 7 hours and 9 minutes from Turbo, the nearest seaport. The transportation infrastructures have, however, considerably improved over the years. Indeed, the transportation time needed to reach Bogota, Cali, or the nearest seaport and port hubs, such as Cartagena, used to take double, triple, or even quadruple the time. Air transportation was the normal connection between Medellín and the outside world due to the city's challenging topographic and geographic dimensions. The *Olaya Herrera* airport opened in 1932 and is located within the city of Medellín. The *Olaya Herrera* airport has, however, limited capacity and is not adapted to large commercial airplanes. In 1985, the *José María Córdova* international airport was inaugurated to allow the landing of larger commercial airplanes and to increase the passenger and cargo capacity and movement. As of 2018, the *José María Córdova* international airport has only 11 international destinations, which means that international travelers often have to take a connecting flight to reach Medellín. This geographic and topographic isolation contributed to nurture the "Paisa culture", which is characterized by the proudness and inward-looking culture of its inhabitants, the elite's sense of paternalism, family, hardworking, and entrepreneurial values, and the kindness and friendly spontaneity of its inhabitant towards the foreigners who express their affections for Medellín and the Paisas. As put by Juan Pablo Ortega, former Ruta N director, "for the MIT faculty and students, the world is a village. For the Paisas, this village is the world" (personal communication, July 7, 2017).

The city of Medellín has experienced from the late 1970s to the early 2000s, a period of extreme violence. In 1991, at the peak of violence, there were 381 homicides for 100,000 inhabitants making the city of Medellín, the most dangerous city in the world (Hylton, 2007). The violence was the outcome of multi-dimensional conflicts between narco-traffickers, right-wing paramilitaries, left-wing insurrectionary militias, criminal gangs, and the state. In the late 1980s and 1990s, the city was a no-go-zone for international visitors, businessmen, and investors except for DEA agents, shady businessmen, and thrill-seekers. The extreme level of violence in Medellín occurred in a period of increasing globalization for most developed and developing countries around the world. The sheer level of violence contributed to further isolate Medellín, at a time when integration to the world economy was imperative to reap the early benefits of the process of globalization. The violence thus hindered the diffusion of extra-regional knowledge into the city.

The industrial, business, and political elites have traditionally been protective of their regional interests by limiting the number of foreign investments in the region. The *Grupo Empresarial Antioqueño* (GEA), a Keiretsu-like conglomerate where Antioquia companies have cross-ownership dubbed *The Other Medellín Cartel*, has since the late 1970s consciously limited the amount of extra-regional investments into the region (Lane, 1996). The GEA includes the largest companies in the Antioquia region and represented around 5.5% of the Colombian GDP in 2008 (Gutiérrez, 2008). Helmsing (1990) argues that the low level of foreign direct investment (FDI) in Antioquia greatly contributed to the stagnation of Antioquian industry. Indeed, foreign companies have favored investing in Cali or Bogotá due to the regionalist attitude of the industrial elite and the region's relatively high labor costs. The limited role of foreign capital in Medellín's industrial success also contributed to a shared sense of pride among the industrial elites and the population. In addition, the protectionist nature of the industrial elite limited the inflow of undesirable competitors, while continuing to expand their operations internationally.

The protectionist nature of the industrial elites was enabled by a shared social and cultural capital. Indeed, the industrial elites come from families that have preserved their wealth for generations, that have developed a close proximity with the public sector to protect their vested interests, that have graduated from the same universities, such as the University of Antioquia, University of the Andes, or EAFIT University; that have country houses (*fincas*) in Rionegro, Retiro, or La Ceja, and that are members of the *Club Unión* and *Club Campestre* (Restrepo Santamaria, 2011). As a result, to be part of the Antioquia elites, one must not only possess the economic but also the social and cultural capital. For instance, Pablo Escobar could not enter the *Club Campestre*, a traditional elite club, despite being far wealthier than any other member.

In summary, the three most important factors that have contributed to isolate Medellín from extra-regional scientific and technological knowledge are: the geographic and topographic dimensions that have nurtured an inward-looking culture; the period of extreme violence in the late 1970s to the 2000s, and the elite's protectionist nature that has reduced foreign direct investments into the region. This relative isolation has not only contributed to reducing the amount of extra-regional knowledge into the region but also regional absorptive capacity. The primary rationale for government intervention was to connect Medellín to extra-regional scientific and technological sources of knowledge to accelerate Medellín's transformation into a knowledge city.

Proantioquia, the GEA's unofficial philanthropic foundation, was the most important actor in the definition of Ruta N's role in the RIS. Indeed, the most important actors in Ruta N's creation have strong links with Proantioquia, and thus indirectly with the GEA. Mayor Alonso Salazar (2008-2011) was backed by Proantioquia, the CTA was created by Proantioquia, and EPM-UNE has historical links with the industrial elite. Additionally, Ruta N's funding and budget largely come from the mandatory transfers of EPM-UNE to the City of Medellín. The spending of EPM-UNE transfers to the City of Medellín is scrutinized to the extent, that large projects using EPM-UNE funds have to be tacitly be approved by the business elite.

Proantioquia (and the GEA) was motivated to create Ruta N for three reasons. The first reason was to promote the region's acquisition of extra-regional scientific and technological knowledge, to connect Medellín with leading innovation hubs, and to make the city visible to leading innovation hubs around the world. In the 1990s, the GEA began to internationalize its activities and to transition towards more service-based and knowledge-based activities. Ruta N is thus the institutional instrument to accelerate this transition. Moreover, Ruta N is serving as an instrument to acquire, diffuse, and assimilate extra-regional scientific and technological knowledge into the region, thus strengthening the regional firms' capacity to compete abroad, while, at the same time, reducing the threat of the arrival of hostile competitors into the region.

The second reason comes from the genuine commitment of the business elite for regional economic development and the promotion of social inclusion. From 1978 to 2015, the GEA, under the leadership of Nicanor Restrepo Santamaría, assumed a paternalist vision aligned with the regional tradition to promote social and economic progress (Calle, 2015; Restrepo Santamaria, 2011). Ruta N's role was also to promote social transformation and inclusion. Since the 1990s, the economic and political elites understood the importance of social inclusion for regional economic development. More importantly, the economic and political elites also understood their roles in the socio-economic crises of the 1980s-1990s that were driven by economic inequality, the lack of public services, informal housing, and the lack of public spaces and, as a result, felt that they owe a historical debt owed to Medellín's poorest neighborhoods and inhabitants (Maclean, 2014).

The third reason comes from the threat posed by the "narco-elite", also known as *"clase emergente"*, to the GEA's vested interests. As argued by Franz (2018), the creation of Ruta N as a public-private partnership can serve as leverage to put pressure on the local government in the case where the local government is not aligned with the interests of the GEA but of competing elite groups, such as the "narco-elite". Indeed, the "narco-elite" have the resources to corrupt the political class, which can hinder regional economic development and Medellín's transformation into a knowledge city (Franz, 2018). The leaks from confidential cables from the US Embassy in Bogotá show that "narco-groups" have indeed been successful at corrupting politicians, public officials, and police forces. Mayor Alonso Salazar actively fought against Luis Pérez who is suspected of having links with the *Oficina de Envigado* (US Embassy, 2008).

"There wasn't an institution promoting innovation and entrepreneurship that we [Proantioquia] think has to be a permanent objective for a city like ours if we want to become more connected in the new competitive realities of Latin America and the world. We shared with the municipal government the importance of structuring a vehicle to support new entrepreneurs, especially entrepreneurs in new businesses, new technologies, new types of products and services, and for globalization" (personal communication, 8 August 2017).

Sources of Funding. Ruta N's funding structure comes from five sources, namely from the city of Medellín, from EPM-UNE, from rents received from the Ruta N building complex, from agreements with partners, and from Ruta N's programs. In 2013, funds also came from the General System of Royalties, which was created in 2011 through the Legislative Act 05 amending the articles 360 and 361 of the Colombian Constitution of 1991. Ruta N was selected by the regional government to manage the General System of Royalties for Antioquia which transferred some funds from the central government to be invested in projects related to Science, Technology, and Innovation (STI) in the region. The General System of Royalties is administered and allocated from Bogotá by the Collegiate Bodies of Administration and Decision (OCAD), which comprises representatives from the local, regional, and central governments. The General System of Royalties works in a three-step manner. First, the Antioquia region is allocated a specific amount of fund through the Science, Technology and Innovation Fund (STIF). Second, Ruta N selects some projects to be funded. Third, the OCAD evaluates and approves Ruta N's projects in terms of their scientific and technological values.

Ruta N's primary source of funding comes from the City of Medellín and EPM-UNE. The City of Medellín is responsible for allocating to Ruta N the resources transferred by EPM-UNE to them. On August 10, 2012, the Medellín's Council adopted the 2011-2021 Science, Technology and Innovation (STI) Plan through the Municipal Agreement 024 of 2012, which seeks to "support, promote, and coordinate STI policies for scientific research, technological development, and innovation in Medellín with the objectives to identify and to create new knowledge-based companies" (Concejo de Medellín, 2012). The second article of the Municipal Agreement 024 of 2012 empowers the Mayor to fund the 2011-2021 Science, Technology and Innovation Plan with at least 7% of the ordinary resources coming from EPM-UNE that are transferred annually to the City of Medellín (Concejo de Medellín, 2012). Moreover, the second article of the Municipal Agreement 024 of 2012 designates Ruta N as the entity in charge of the implementation of the 2011-2021 STI Plan (Concejo de Medellín, 2012). The City of Medellín has, however, never followed the Municipal Agreement 024 in allocating 7% of the EPM ordinary profits to Ruta N. It has systematically allocated less, since the City of Medellín started with to directly implement programs related to STI with the Secretary of Economic Development. After the election of Mayor Federico Gutiérrez (2016-2019), Ruta N's funding from the municipal government decreased by 60% due to the Gutiérrez administration's intention to implement STI projects directly at the Secretary of Economic Development and to prioritize other areas, such as security.

Ruta N's model aimed to make the organization as financially independent as possible from the City of Medellín to limit the influence of political changes on Ruta N's strategy. In addition to the funding from its partners, namely the City of Medellín and EPM-UNE, Ruta N receives income from multiple sources. Since the opening of the Ruta N building complex, Ruta N receives rents from the companies and startups located in the soft-landing platform as well as rents from commercial and retail spaces located in the building. Moreover, Ruta N receives financial compensation from bilateral agreements, such as from the University at Wisconsin-Madison, Bancoldex, Bio Nano Center Limited, the Historic and Touristic District of Santa Marta, and the Health Institute of the Nariño Department (Ruta N, 2016, p. 92). Ruta N also receives financial compensations from the organized workshops, short courses, and training, such as at the ViveLab, Laboratorio de Creación, or the Great Pact for the Innovation. Finally, Ruta N receives financial compensation from consulting services to clients, and from selling digital animations and web services. Despite the financial model to make the organization financially independent from the City of Medellín, political interference is still a source of concern.

"I really worry on the political dimension of Ruta N. Until now we have had excellent directors, but it is a politician who selects the director and I am worried that the next Mayor be a Luis Pérez or someone like him. The political interference in Ruta N can be quite strong which means that the entity can serve the Mayor at the political and economic levels" (personal communication, 24 July 2017).

CHAPTER 10

Ruta N and New Industrial Regional Path Development.

The regional innovation agency (RIA), Ruta N, has the mission to support new industrial regional path development and to promote structural change in the economy. Indeed, Ruta N's primary objective is to support Medellín's economic transformation from an industrial into a knowledge city. The RIA was thus mandated to promote the upgrading of traditional industrial activities into more knowledge-based and service-based activities. This mandate comes from the lessons learned from Medellín's economic history. In the 1970s and 1980s, Medellín experienced a situation of cognitive and political lock-ins of its industrial sector, which ultimately led to the city's worst economic and social period in its history. In the 1990s, the city's economic structure was reorganized towards more service-based and knowledge-based activities from the GEA understanding that lasting economic growth and social well-being would only come from developing strong and growing knowledge-based and service-based activities.

As pointed out by a Google Manager in a talk at Ruta N, "the Paisa is famous for its entrepreneurial spirit, and it is the view that we have had for the last 50 years. No large company, however, has emerged in Medellín in the past couple of decades. That is what Ruta N is trying to make happen through bringing together young entrepreneurs who want to solve global and regional problems" (as cited in Ruta N, 2013). The RIA has pursued new industrial path development in six different sectors, including path branching and path creation. The sectors that have been selected for path branching, which are sectors that already existed in the region but that needed to be upgraded, are, ICT, health, and energy. The sectors that have been selected for path creation, which are sectors that did not exist in the region are, nanotechnology, digital animation and video games, and to a lesser extent biotechnology.

Ruta N is in charge of implementing the Science, Technology, and Innovation (STI) Plan 2011-2021, which was drafted in 2010 in a collective effort involving more than 250 regional leaders, namely entrepreneurs, business leaders, policymakers, and academics to identify new industrial path development. The STI Plan has the objective "to promote and coordinate policies to support research and scientific, technological and innovative development in Medellín, with a view towards the identification and exploitation of new knowledge-based businesses" as well as to transform Medellín into the "most innovative city in Latin America" (Pineda & Scheel, 2011). The STI Plan was adopted as a public policy by the Medellín Council through the Municipal Agreement 024 of 2012, which granted, for the period 2011-2021, 7% of EPM ordinary profits to Ruta N to conduct investments and to support companies and research organizations in science, technology, and innovation. The STI Plan targets three sectors, ICT, energy, and health, which were selected on the basis of potential growth and prior capabilities.

Ruta N's strategy to support new industrial path development has heavily relied on acquiring, exploiting, and diffusing extra-regional technological and scientific knowledge. The degree to which extra-regional knowledge was acquired depended on whether the new industrial path development already existed in the region. For path branching, extra-regional knowledge has been acquired to respond to specific weaknesses in ICT, health, and energy to strengthen local capacities. The extra-regional knowledge has been acquired to allow the process of recombination with local capacities and thus to facilitate the generation of technological innovations. The acquisition of extra-regional knowledge reduces technological lock-ins and strengthens the capacity of the new industrial path development to move towards new technological opportunities. For path creation, digital animation and video games and the nanotechnology sector have heavily relied on extra-regional knowledge to build capacities and extra-regional actors to implement programs.

New Industrial Path Development	2007	2009	2011	2013	2015	2017	Percentage Change (2007-2017)
Path Branching							
ICT	2251	2090	2392	2811	3704	4257	89,12
Energy	884	818	1014	632	847	915	3,51
Health	1173	1254	1502	3082	3910	4215	259,34
Path Creation							
Digital Animation and Video Game*	_	_	_	338	522	616	
Nanotechnology+	_	_	_	28	44	60	

* The digital animation and video game sector includes: software development, video postproduction, graphic design, and audiovisual creation corresponding to ISIC 5820, 5912, 7410, and 9004.
+ Nanotechnology includes the actors participating in the regional innovation initiative in nanotechnology.

Table 2. Number of Companies in the New Industrial Path Development. Source: Economic Research Unit, Chamber of Commerce of Medellín for Antioquia.

A Knowledge Broker. Ruta N has supported new industrial path development by working as a knowledge broker in the RIS. Indeed, the RIA has played the role of an intermediary organization between extra-regional actors and actors within the RIS with the objective of strengthening the capacities in science, technology, and innovation of the actors in the RIS. In supporting new industrial path development, Ruta N has been performing three primary functions. First, Ruta N screens the weaknesses in the RIS and identifies the actors in the RIS to strengthen, such as private companies, public institutions, universities, technological development centers, civil society, and so on. Second, Ruta N identifies the potential regional or extra-regional actor with the capacity to strengthen the targeted actor. Third, the regional or extra-regional actor with the capacity implements a program to transfer that capacity to the targeted actor. In the words of Elkin Echeverrí, director of the Forecasting and Planning working area, "what Ruta N tries to do is: to observe the world, to determine what the regional innovation system is missing, to find the organizations with the solution, to bring them into the system, and to inject that capacity. The organizations do not come to Medellín to give a conference but have contracts to stay 6 months, 8 months, or a year" (Ruta N, 2015).

As a result, Ruta N's primary role is to act as a knowledge broker between the actors that possess the knowledge and the actors that require the knowledge. For the RIA, the brokerage of extra-regional knowledge has three objectives: first, to improve the capacity of the RIS to acquire, absorb, and diffuse extra-regional knowledge; second, to connect Medellín and Ruta N to relevant innovation hubs around the world, such as Boston, Austin, Silicon Valley, Israel, or Cambridge, to generate formal and informal networks between regional and international actors; and third, to improve the visibility of Medellín and Ruta N as a relevant innovation system in the world. The collaboration with international actors has, for Ruta N, three objectives. The first objective is to transfer knowledge to the regional actors in the regional innovation system. Horacio Vélez, CEO of UNE, pointed out, "we are seeking alliances, not partnerships, which is not the same thing, we are looking to bring to the city knowledge from all over the world from world class actors such as HP, Huawei" (Ruta N, 2010b). The second objective is to connect Ruta N and Medellín to innovation hubs around the world, such as Boston, Austin, Silicon Valley, Israel, or Cambridge, and thus to generate networks between regional and international actors. The third objective is to position Ruta N and Medellín as a significant innovation system in the world.

A Knowledge Gatekeeper. In addition to brokering knowledge, Ruta N monitors the progress of each of its programs, especially when it involves an extra-regional implementing actor, thus playing the role of a knowledge gatekeeper. As a public knowledge gatekeeper in the RIS, Ruta N is performing three primary functions. First, the RIA is continuously monitoring best-practices in RIS around the world. Second, the RIA acts as a node in the RIS that is exposed to weaknesses in the RIS and best practices around the world. Third, the RIA has the capacity to assist extra-regional actors in translating the extra-regional knowledge to actors in the RIS. In contrast to knowledge brokers that only act as an intermediary in the acquisition of knowledge between two actors, knowledge gatekeepers support the translation of the knowledge, and thus facilitate its absorption into the RIS. Indeed, Ruta N monitors the programs implemented by extra-regional actors to ensure that the knowledge is effectively transferred and is relevant to the local context. In the case of Ruta N, its role as knowledge gatekeeper is conducted through supporting the "tropicalization" of the extra-regional knowledge, that is, through the hybridization of tacit extra-regional knowledge with local knowledge. Ruta N is thus the institutional arrangement and regional innovation governance structure that aims to respond to the two most significant challenges in establishing successful global pipelines. The first one relates to the identification of the pipelines to tap into (Bathelt, Malmberg, & Maskell, 2004). The second one relates to the translation and assimilation of the information arriving through the pipelines.

Tropicalizing Extra-Regional Knowledge. The act of "tropicalizing knowledge," coined due to the city's geographic location between the tropics, refers to the adaptation of the extra-regional knowledge to Medellín's context, culture, and existing capacities to better facilitate its absorption by the actors of the RIS. Indeed, Ruta N provides continuous support for extra-regional actors, mainly from developed countries, that are implementing programs "to tropicalize" their programs to the context of the city. Ruta N's knowledge gatekeeper role is conducted by supporting the "tropicalization" of the extra-regional knowledge, that is, through the hybridization of tacit extra-regional knowledge with the local knowledge. The public knowledge gatekeeper, Ruta N, has three roles: the acquisition of extra-regional knowledge, the "tropicalization" of that knowledge, and the diffusion of that knowledge into the RIS.

Every month Ruta N organizes the Ruta N Open House event to connect entrepreneurs and students with some of the main actors in the RIS, such as *CREAME, ANDI, Parque E, Social Atom,* and *Ruta N.*

During the Ruta N Open House held on August 31, 2017, the speaker from Ruta N told the diverse audience, including students, local residents, knowledge workers, and entrepreneurs how Ruta N defines innovation, "we took the definition of innovation from the Oslo Manual that is used by the most developed and the most competitive cities in the world and adapted it to our context in Medellín in order for it to make sense to us." For Ruta N, innovation is defined as "a new idea and billing", in other words, the generation of economic value-added to the exploitation of a new idea (Ruta N, 2014). Ruta N in defining innovation was, as a result, "tropicalizing" extra-regional knowledge, that is, adapting extra-regional knowledge to make it relevant and understandable to the audience. This event illustrates Ruta N's role and mission as a knowledge gatekeeper to improve the region's absorptive capacity to extra-regional knowledge.

Ruta N's knowledge gatekeeper role "tropicalizing knowledge" was highlighted in many interviews.

> "Our [Ruta N] greatest effort was to ensure that the knowledge was relevant to the context of the city. That is, not doing the program in the same way it is done in Austin, Texas. That what we did with IC^2, we were super demanding with them and they were quite surprised, telling us, they always were transferring the methodology in the same way. We told them, let's check if it has meaning for the conditions of Medellín, Colombia, and Latin America. We were like partners, building together the program" (personal communication, July 7, 2017).

> "In 2015, we [Ruta N] contracted the Spanish firm Tecnalia to design a business model for the National Centre for Nanotechnology. The business model was very well done but had one important flaw in that it was very European centered, especially in its financing structure. What we did is, take part of the model and adapt it to our context" (personal communication, July 17, 2018).

Ruta N has, however, faced some difficulties in "tropicalizing knowledge" due to a lack of internal capabilities in contextualizing extra-regional knowledge and a misunderstanding of its core knowledge gatekeeping role. In its infancy, Ruta N has also misjudged the innovative capacities of many actors in the RIS and thus their capacities to effectively absorb extra-regional knowledge, which, as a result, limited the policy effectiveness of brokering extra-regional knowledge.

"They [Ruta N] brought very skilled experts in different fields of innovation. I remember well the Israelis who came to Medellín to give a course that was so complex for us that the entrepreneurs were saying, 'I don't understand and don't have the capacity to assimilate what they are offering'" (personal communication, August 3, 2018).

"The program led by the Founder Institute brought really successful entrepreneurs from the Silicon Valley. The local entrepreneurs, however, were unprepared to really take advantage of the program and the mentors from the Founder Institute didn't have knowledge of the local innovation system. I used to tell my boss that the program was like having a Renault car with Ferrari tires. The Founder Institute didn't want to adapt their program to the local needs, saying that they were conducting the same program all over the world in the same way and didn't have to adapt their program. We thus decided to hire the Argentine company NXTP Labs for the next version of the program since they had more experience in Latin America" (personal communication, July 28, 2017).

Diffusing Knowledge into the Regional Innovation System. In addition to tropicalizing knowledge, Ruta N has devised programs to diffuse the acquired knowledge into the RIS. As shown by Morrison, Rabelloti, and Zirulia (2013), global pipelines are most beneficial to RIS with high-quality local buzz and weak knowledge endowment. Ruta N is supporting interactions to diffuse the extra-regional knowledge between different actors of the RIS. The programs aim to foster face-to-face interactions and virtual face-to-face interactions to create a sense of "local buzz" to diffuse knowledge between different actors in the RIS. Ruta N promotes "local buzz" through programs that specifically encourage repeated face-to-face and virtual interactions and through the creation of specific urban amenities, namely the innovation center and the innovation district.

Ruta N is also implementing urban transformations that promote face-to-face interactions between different actors in the RIS. Indeed, one of the objectives of the Ruta N innovation center and the Medellínnovation District is to encourage repeated face-to-face interactions and the spread of tacit knowledge by clustering different innovative actors of the RIS in a high-quality and high amenities urban district. The Medellínnovation District aims to regenerate a 172-hectare area around the Ruta N building complex, which serves as an anchor space for the innovation district. Indeed, the Ruta N building complex is an innovation center housing national and international startups, Ruta N, research centers, universities, and private companies (see Morisson, 2018). The urban component aims to facilitate repeated face-to-face interactions, serendipitous encounters, the spread of tacit knowledge, local buzz, and ultimately the collaboration between widely diverse innovative actors located in the innovation center and the innovation district.

Ruta N's Strategy for Supporting the Innovation Process. Ruta N creates programs to support new industrial path development by addressing weaknesses in the Technology Readiness Levels (TRLs) of the specific targeted sector or subsector. TRLs are "indicators of the maturity level of particular technologies" (European Commission, 2016). In the literature, there are nine TRLs ranging from TRL 1 being the lowest to TRL 9 being the highest. Ruta N has used the TRLs in many different programs as heuristics to devise programs, and as metrics to evaluate projects and to provide funding. The TRL is used as a measurement system that provides a systematic understanding of a technology status in the entire innovation process. In Ruta N's strategy, TRL 0, the idea, and TRL 10, the internationalization, can be added to the traditional Technology Readiness Levels (see Figure 1).

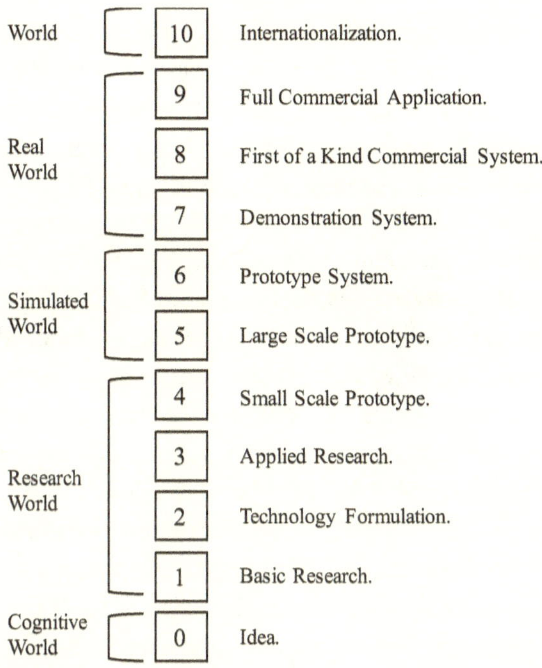

Figure 1. Technology Readiness Levels (TRLs) adapted by the author from the European Commission (2016).

Ruta N has devised and implemented numerous programs to address weaknesses in the RIS's TRL either at the level of the RIS, at the level of a sector, or at the level of a subsector with the end goal of supporting the technological innovation process. In the language of Ruta N, this activity refers to "*cerrar brechas*", or literally to close gaps. The activity of "*cerrar brechas*" can be done at the level of the RIS, at the level of a sector, or at the level of a subsector. Ruta N has devised and implemented programs to upgrade the RIS capacities at specific TRLs that either target one element of the TRL, such as Passport N and the Market Access

Network, to support local actors in their internationalization process (TRL 10). Ruta N has also created programs to support local actors in moving up along the TRL scale, such as the Pre-Acceleration for Startups (TRL 4 to TRL 8) or the program InLab2Market (TRL 2 to TRL 8). In devising new programs, Ruta N monitors the current significant weaknesses, or *"brechas"*, in the RIS and will design a specific program to intervene in the RIS to bring the needed capacities into the RIS. The innovation process is, however, not linear. Interactions between widely diverse actors in the RIS allow the diffusion knowledge and best-practices, which would enable for recombination and thus reaching higher TRLs.

Ruta N has designed and implemented programs that are embedded into a broader and more complex strategy. It strengthens the technological innovation process with the following strategy. First, the Science, Technology, and Innovation Observatory provides a technology watch and competitive intelligence, screening potential opportunities for the local actors in the regional innovation system not only in the three strategic sectors identified in the STI Plan—ICT, health, and energy—but also in emerging markets. The STI Observatory provides local actors with potential opportunities at the early stage of the innovation process, namely the Technology Readiness Levels ranging from 1 to 4. Indeed, the STI Observatory allows actors to redirect research efforts into specific technological trajectories in which the city can reach a competitive position. Second, Ruta N identifies, through public calls, innovative actors that can carry out specific scientific and technological activities beneficial to the RIS. Third, Ruta N devises and implements programs on two strategic axes. The first type of programs aims to strengthen the scientific and technological capacities of innovative actors to reach higher TRLs. Ruta N's programs that target technological and scientific capabilities have relied on the identification of weaknesses in regional capacities within the TRL framework, on the identification of regional and extra-regional actors possessing the needed knowledge to allow the regional actors to move up along the TRL, and on the knowledge tropicalization to facilitate the knowledge absorption into the RIS. Moreover, Ruta N has also created programs to promote interactions between innovative actors in the RIS to facilitate the diffusion of that knowledge. Ruta N has also provided through co-financing, lending, and subsidies mechanisms funding to the regional actors to support them in moving along the TRL and in becoming more innovative. In addition to promoting technological innovations, Ruta N has created programs to affect the evolution of the socio-institutional structure to the novel techno-economic paradigm.

Facilitating the Co-evolution of the Socio-Institutional Structure. Medellín is transitioning from an industrial city towards a more service-based and knowledge-based city. The conceptual framework stresses the role of the entrepreneurial region in supporting radical socio-institutional changes for two reasons. First, the entrepreneurial region has to align the socio-institutional structure with the new industrial path development to support the RIS' absorptive capacity to fully exploit extra-regional knowledge. Second, the entrepreneurial region has to limit transitional failure resulting from the structural change in the economy. Structural change in the regional economy implies rapid path creation and path destruction that affects the socio-institutional structure, which, in turn, through cumulative causation will affect future path development. The socio-institutional structure refers to the evolutionary structures that co-evolve with the techno-economic structure. The socio-institutional structure involves three knowledge-driven structures: (i) the social structure that refers to informal institutions, (ii) the organizational structure that refers to organizational features within private organizations, and (iii) the institutional structure that refers to the organizations that implement and/or devise formal institutions.

Programs to accelerate the co-evolution of the social structure with the novel techno-economic paradigm were devised by the innovation culture working area to foster in "the civil society specific attitudes towards innovation" (personal communication, August 24, 2017). Medellín's residents, or Paisas, are known for their inward-looking culture. As pointed out, "for the MIT faculty and students, the world is a village. For the Paisas, this village is the world" (personal communication, July 7, 2017). Programs have targeted residents of Medellín, university students, and middle and high school students. Some of the programs intended to affect the evolution of the social structure are, for instance, the Ruta N's Innovation Awards, Horizons, the Medellínnovation Festival, Startup Weekend, and N-Lab. Ruta N's Innovation Awards is a program intended to reward innovators in Medellín to position them as aspirational leaders for other actors in the region. The program Horizons exposed public middle and high school students to high-demand skills in robotics, engineering, and nanotechnology. Horizons aimed "to inspire students to form new imaginaries, which can foster new attitudes, so that the students can internalize their roles in the innovation process" (personal communication, August 24, 2017). The program Horizons aimed to generate aspiration for middle and high school students to pursue science, technology, engineering, and mathematics (STEM) careers. The Medellínnovation Festival was a week-long event with multiple events, workshops, and conferences across the city to diffuse innovation concepts and an innovation culture to the civil society. The program Startup Weekend aims to influence university students to pursue entrepreneurship and to create their startups. The programs N-Lab and Innovation Challenge aimed to connect students with private companies to answer specific challenges and to promote entrepreneurship. Ruta N has conducted several communication campaigns, such as "if you imagine it, it is possible" or "to innovate, it comes from people like you", around the city to diffuse an innovation culture.

Ruta N has created programs to accelerate the co-evolution of the organizational structure with the novel techno-economic paradigm. Programs have targeted large companies, SMEs, and startups. Some of the programs intended to affect the social structure are Innovation is for Everyone, Innovation Seminars, Innovation Managers, Innovation Management, SCRUM, the Great Pact for Innovation, Social Lab and Intellectual Property. The programs Innovation is for Everyone, Innovation Seminars, and Innovation Managers aimed to diffuse and to democratize key concepts of technological innovation to the employees of private companies. Innovation Managers targeted 221 companies and provided training in methodology, best practices, knowledge concepts, and tools for 8 months to foster innovative business strategies. The Argentine company Kleer provided training to companies to accelerate software development through the SCRUM methodology. The Swedish company Idealaboratoriet led the program Innovation Management to promote an entrepreneurial culture within private companies through lateral and agile thinking methodologies. In 2014, the Great Pact for Innovation was signed by more than 1400 local actors to participate in the innovation effort for Medellín to reach 3% of its GDP in R&D spending in 2021. The pact was widely celebrated and communicated as a collective effort to achieve "a common vision of the future" (Headrik, 1988, p. 13). In the social lab program, Boston College transferred methodologies to large companies to adopt corporate social responsibility practices. Finally, the program in intellectual property, CATI, provides a methodology to identify within companies potential patentable innovations and to promote a culture favorable to the protection of intellectual property. The common objective of the programs is to transform the companies' organizational structure into one structure favorable to a culture of continuous innovation and entrepreneurial thinking.

> "When we did Innovation Seminars, we were at a moment of Ruta N's history when we wanted to democratize innovation, that is, to have everyone understand innovation. It was very large groups in which we taught face-to-face seminars about innovation, what it is, how to do it, but because our purpose was to democratize, we decided to virtualize the course with the program Innovation is for Everyone" (personal communication, August 9, 2018).

> "We looked at the different innovation indicators of the OECD, and we saw the gap between Medellín and the different countries of the OECD. We won't close the gap by creating many programs

but by giving the responsibility to others, so the Great Pact for the Innovation was like a symbol" (personal communication, July 25, 2017).

Ruta N has created programs to accelerate the co-evolution of the institutional structure with the novel techno-economic paradigm. Programs have targeted the city of Medellín, educational institutions, linkage organizations, and technological research centers. The institutional structure of the city of Medellín has been affected by programs such as Citiesfor.life, MiMedellín, MEData, the Fast-Track Institute, and the Innovation Laboratory for Government. Citiesfor.life was an event held in Medellín in 2015 where international urban experts and mayors were invited to exchange public best practices. The web platform Citiesfor.life was launched to enable cities to exchange best practices for urban challenges. MiMedellín is an open innovation web platform that allows citizens to participate in co-creating urban projects responding to the city's challenges. The program MEData aims to foster a data-driven governance strategy for the city of Medellín. The Fast-Track Institute is a spinoff from the Singular University in San Francisco and seeks to find exponential solutions to urban challenges in transportation, health, and sustainability for the city of Medellín. Educational institutions, namely universities and high schools, have been affected by programs such as SCRUM, Acceleration Program, Innovacampus, Spinoff Colombia, and Generation N. The Argentine company Kleer transferred the SCRUM methodology to disrupt the education sector through ICT. Cambridge University led the acceleration program to mentor local universities in developing disruptive projects. The program Innovacampus aimed to foster innovative capacities in local universities through the exchange of best practices with German universities. Through the program Spinoff Colombia, Ruta N has enabled the adoption of a national policy facilitating the creation of university spinoffs. Additionally, the program Spinoff Colombia supports university research centers through a methodology in bringing research inventions to market. The program Generation N aims to train high school teachers in project-based learning as a pedagogical tool for teaching STEM classes. Linkage institutions, including Ruta N, have been affected through the Diagnostic for Regional Innovation Systems and the program Innovation Management for Institutions. The OECD and T2 Venture Capital provided consulting to recommend improvements in programs to build a stronger regional innovation system. Innovation Management for institutions aims to generate capacities for linkage institutions to offer consulting services. Finally, the Monterrey Institute of Technology led the program Encurso to provide health professionals at technological research centers a methodology to conduct efficient clinical trials.

"In the Innovation Laboratory for Government, we want to have the entities of the local government, Secretaries, and decentralized entities, start thinking about innovation. Citizens often perceive the government as a very archaic and massive thing. We went there to motivate the Secretaries to start implementing innovative processes, connecting them with citizens to listen to them and to prioritize goals, and most importantly to find solutions" (personal communication, August 3, 2018).

The socio-institutional structure has considerably evolved in the past decade. From the interviews conducted with expert stakeholders in the regional innovation system, the role of Ruta N in supporting socio-institutional change has been positive. Ruta N has been more successful in transforming the socio-organizational structure than the institutional structure. In the past decade, the socio-organizational structure has evolved towards a more positive perception of innovation and entrepreneurship, as pointed out: "Ruta N has been successful in generating in a short period a critical mass of persons and companies interested in topics related to innovation and entrepreneurship" (personal communication, August 22, 2018). The organizational structure has evolved to more entrepreneurial and investment attitudes to innovations thanks to the successful transfer from Ruta N of methodologies to private companies. For the institutional structure, while "Ruta N is an institutional innovation", Ruta N has failed to collaborate with institutional actors in the RIS due to its strong paternalistic vision towards other actors in the RIS. Moreover, the non-alignment of some public organizations with the GEA's interests led to resistance to changes promoted by Ruta N, which is seen by those public organizations as too aligned with the GEA. Ruta N has, however, been successful in generating more citizens' participation and co-creation with the program MiMedellín and more recently with the Innovation Laboratory for Government.

CHAPTER 11

Ruta N's Unique Role in the RIS.

Ruta N has two primary roles to perform in its RIS. Ruta N's first role is that of a public knowledge gatekeeper "tropicalizing knowledge" to support new industrial path development. Ruta N's second role is to accelerate the co-evolution of the socio-institutional structure with the new techno-economic paradigm. Ruta N has the role to monitor extra-regional best-practices and tropicalize those practices to Medellín's and Colombia's context. Regions on the knowledge periphery are less exposed to knowledge from regions at the technological frontier, and, as a result, need interventions. The creation of Ruta N in Medellín is the type of intervention that aims to increase extra-regional knowledge flows and to improve the RIS's absorption capacity. In contrast with other knowledge gatekeepers, such as leader firms or universities, in which a lag persists in leaking knowledge, the public knowledge gatekeepers directly transfer the extra-regional knowledge to the actors in the RIS. This role of the RIA is sometimes difficult to understand for experts coming from regions in the knowledge core.

> "When we have people coming from abroad, especially from Europe, in the meetings I have with them, they don't understand well Ruta N. Probably because the levels of development are different. For instance, with the Germans, they were asking me but 'what is Ruta N? What do they do?'" (personal communication, July 12, 2017).

In addition to playing the role of a public knowledge gatekeeper, Ruta N has, over the years, developed internal capacities to create and implement its own programs as well as to influence national innovation policies. The programs Innovation Managers, MiMedellín, the Great Pact for the Innovation, the Living Lab, and the Innovation Laboratory, among others, have been created and implemented by Ruta N with little help from national and international actors. The programs that have been developed from Ruta N leadership have even spurred national policies and strategies. The national strategy "Vive Digital" and the "ViveLab" to develop national capacities for the digital economy spurred by the Ministry of ICT and Colciencias, was initially promoted by Ruta N. The program Spinoff Colombia enabled changes in national policy that allowed public universities in Colombia to create spinoffs and professors to receive royalties from the creation of the spinoff. Spinoff Colombia is similar to the Bayh-Dole Act implemented in the United States in the late 1980s. The program Spinoff Colombia offers support from experts in the legal incorporation and accompaniment of the Spinoff.

The Evolution of Science, Technology, and Innovation. Medellín is slowly transitioning from being an industrial city towards becoming a service-based and knowledge-based city. In 2004, Medellín started a process of technological catch-up with regions in the knowledge core. This technological catch-up process accelerated since 2013 showing that public policies have to be consistent for many years in order to deliver concrete results. As highlighted in the interviews, although Medellín is still far from having caught up with regions in the knowledge core, this technological catch-up process has accelerated in the past years. R&D and STI spending in the City of Medellín have reached 2.14% of the GDP in 2017, thus becoming Colombian city investing most in innovation (Ruta N, 2018b). The technological catch-up process is felt not only at the scientific and technological level but also at the level of the socio-institutional structure.

> "Max Planck, Fraunhofer from Germany are now here in Medellín, the University of Wisconsin is also here, we thought it was going to take 20 years to bring those organizations, but they are now here" (personal communication, July 27, 2017).

> "Every Friday, the *Cacaos* [the CEOs of the largest companies in Medellín who are part of the GEA] were meeting at

Proantioquia and they were telling us in 2009, 'what you are doing is very important for the region, we don't want it to have anything to do with us, but do it'. In 2009 and 2010, these large companies didn't have a department in charge of innovation but today all of them have one. This does not mean that it has anything to do with Ruta N, but that Ruta N was the first to speak about the necessity to innovate" (personal communication, July 7, 2017).

"Private companies are now willing to take risks with entrepreneurs, which was not the case 10 years ago. When we were doing courses in business models 10 years ago, the entrepreneurs came with very traditional business models. Today, thanks to all the work that has been done, entrepreneurs are looking to generate high economic value-added in their industries" (personal communication, August 22, 2018).

"Medellín has had a relatively consistent strategy with efforts coming from the public and private sector. The early conversation that we started to have in science, technology, and innovation for the last 15 years has led to the fact that Medellín is now recognized in the national context and in some cities in Latin America" (personal communication, 23 August 2018).

The different indicators that can be used to measure Science, Technology, and Innovation, either in inputs, namely R&D and STI spending, and outputs, namely patents and trademarks registered, have considerably increased in the Antioquia Region (see Table 3). Indeed, between 2009 and 2016, R&D spending as a percentage of the GDP has increased by 50%, compared with 42% in Colombia; STI Spending as a percentage of GDP has increased by 68%, compared with 58% in Colombia; the number of patents registered has increased by 420%, compared with 372% in Colombia, and the number of trademarks registered has increased by 124%, compared with 69% in Colombia. Moreover, the Antioquia Region has closed the innovation divergence and even surpassed Bogotá in R&D and STI spending. The Antioquia region has also diverged greatly from Valle del Cauca Region, where Cali is located. Moreover, the number of trademarks registered in Antioquia has increased more than in Bogotá D. C., Cali, and Colombia as whole. Trademarks can be used as an indicator for measuring innovation and industrial change (Mendonça, Pereira, & Godinho, 2004), and more specifically, service innovation (Flikkema, De Man, & Castaldi, 2014).

Indicators	Regions	2001	2009	2016	Percentage Change (2001-2016)
R&D spending as pecentage of GDP	Antioquia	0,26	0,38	0,57	119,2
	Bogotá D. C.	0,23	0,32	0,35	52,2
	Valle del Cauca	0,1	0,12	0,15	50,0
	Colombia	0,13	0,19	0,27	107,7
STI spending as percentage of GDP	Antioquia	0,47	0,74	1,24	163,8
	Bogotá D. C.	0,63	0,91	1,05	66,7
	Valle del Cauca	0,41	0,32	0,45	9,8
	Colombia	0,34	0,45	0,71	108,8
Number of local patents registered	Antioquia	6	24	124	1966,7
	Bogotá D. C.	47	63	189	302,1
	Valle del Cauca	8	7	46	475,0
	Colombia	73	126	545	646,6
Number of Trademarks registered	Antioquia	1404	2780	3143	123,9
	Bogotá D. C.	4047	6733	6639	64,0
	Valle del Cauca	883	1398	1397	58,2
	Colombia	16216	22224	27356	68,7

Table 3. Key Innovation Indicators. Source: Superintendencia de Industria y Comercio (2018) and OCyT (2018).

This does not mean that we can infer from the indicators that Ruta N has had a causal effect on Antioquia's innovative capacity. They do, however, show that since the creation of Ruta N, the Antioquia Region has greatly diverged from its initial trajectory by becoming more innovative in terms of measured inputs and outputs. They show that Ruta

N is part of a long-term process that has accelerated Medellín's regional transformation. Moreover, the increasing number of trademarks registered shows that Medellín is increasingly becoming more service-based.

Ruta N as an example of best-practice is, however, nuanced. The regional innovation agency is a classic example of policy running ahead of theory, which has led to many difficulties and misunderstandings in performing its main activities. Indeed, Ruta N has experienced some difficulties in performing its activities due to an inward-looking organizational structure, a lack of internal capabilities, and the misunderstanding of some of its core activities. Ruta N has perceived itself as a startup rather than a public organization, which has led to two major problems. First, Ruta N started to see itself as the city's innovation planner and started to compete with other actors in the RIS. Second, Ruta N failed to collaborate enough with other actors in the RIS and has relied too much on internal capacities and on learning-by-doing following a process of trial-and-error. This has led Ruta N to misjudge the existing innovative capacities of the actors in the RIS and thus to design an offer that didn't have a demand.

Ruta N also faced some difficulties in "tropicalizing" knowledge due to a lack of internal capabilities to translate extra-regional knowledge and due to a misunderstanding of its role as a knowledge gatekeeper. In its infancy, Ruta N also misjudged the innovative capacities of many actors in the RIS and thus their capacities to effectively absorb extra-regional knowledge, which resulted in limiting the policy effectiveness of brokering extra-regional knowledge into the RIS. In the diffusion process, Ruta N, identifying itself as a start-up, created multiple web platforms; Brainbook, SUNN, MiMedellín, and Cities for Life. Brainbook and SUNN were extremely expensive and require a network effect to be widely adopted, which will be unlikely. In addition, Ruta N has over-communicated on its potential future impact and excluded other actors in the RIS while demonstrating few concrete results, which has led to resentment from other actors in the RIS. Finally, in the evaluation process,

Ruta N has failed to consistently and systematically monitor its impacts and effects at the system level, at the agency level, and at the program level, thus reinforcing organizational inefficiencies through unchecked negative feedback loops.

"In the years 2009 to 2014, Ruta N distracted itself in its strategy and it seemed that it was doing everything. It was difficult to understand the strategic role of Ruta N and because in the city there are private venture capital companies, start-up accelerators, start-up incubators, technological development centers, and research groups, it generated a lot of conflicts between the different actors, nothing alarming, but a lack of coordination and a lot of rivalries between the different actors in the innovation ecosystem. Later, another mistake was that Ruta N declared itself as the innovation planner of the ecosystem and this is an enormous mistake because nobody can organize the innovation ecosystem" (personal communication, August 16, 2018).

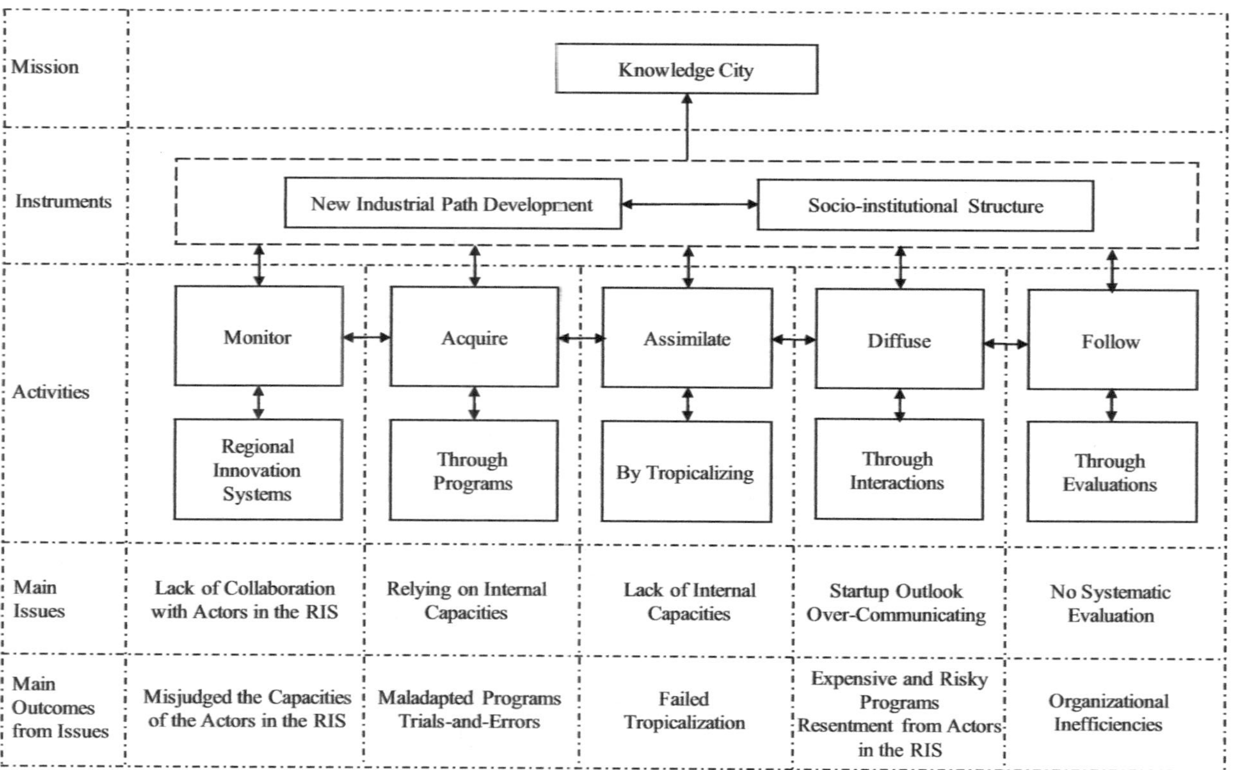

Figure 2. Ruta N's mission, instruments, and activities. Source: own design.

113

Part III

The Entrepreneurial Region Toolkit –

Creating Regional Innovation Agencies in

Regions on the Knowledge Periphery

CHAPTER 12

The Framework for the Regional Innovation Agency.

Regional Innovation Agencies for Regions in the Knowledge Periphery. Regions located on the knowledge periphery could benefit from a regional innovation governance structure and institutional arrangement similar to Ruta N. These regions are geographically remote from the main sources of scientific and technological knowledge. Regions in the knowledge core can have for proxy, regions with significant patenting activities, such as the Top-100 cluster by patent filing in the world, regions that are geographically proximate (within a 200 kilometers radius) to the Top-100 cluster by patent filing in the world, and the regions receiving significant knowledge flows from regions in the Top-100 cluster by patent filing in the world (Bergquist, Fink, & Raffo, 2017). In contrast with core regions, regions on the knowledge periphery have limited extra-regional knowledge linkages, knowledge infrastructures, and capacity to absorb that extra-regional knowledge (Grillitsch & Nilsson, 2015). As a result, global cities and innovation hubs would not benefit from such a regional innovation governance structure and institutional arrangement since they already possess a large and diverse knowledge base allowing the generation of new industrial path development from path-dependent market-forces.

Regional innovation systems located on the knowledge periphery would most benefit from a public organization, like Ruta N, since they lack the required extra-regional knowledge flows to upgrade not only the regions' technological and scientific capabilities but also the regions' socio-institutional structure. Regional innovation systems that would benefit the most from the creation of a regional innovation agency are: first, regions that have been extremely isolated due to embargoes or extreme violence, such as, for example, regions in Cuba, Mexico, Venezuela in Latin America, instable regions in Africa, or Libya in North

Africa or Syria and Iran in the Middle East. Second, the regions that have been at the periphery of the world economy, such as regions with second-tier cities in Latin America, Central Asia, Africa, India, and Southeast Asia. Third, regions that are undergoing structural change in their economics, from industrial to knowledge-based, such as regions in Western Europe, Eastern Europe, and Russia. Fourth, the peripheral regions of the European Union that have increasingly diverged from the knowledge core, such as regions in Southern Europe, South Italy (for instance, Bari, Cagliari, Catania, Naples, and Palermo would be good candidates), some regions in Spain, Greece, and Portugal.

> "People admire how an entity [Ruta N] in just 6 years has managed to transform its ecosystem, something that has not worked in any other part of Latin America. Policymakers from Ivory Coast, from Senegal, came to look at the model, and they told me, 'look, we are a former colony of France, and they help us to come to France, but coming here, I think that what is happening in Medellín and in Ruta N is much closer to the way I see the world than what they told me in France'" (personal communication, 27 July 2017).

A RIA is a place-based and place-sensitive policy-strategy that is not a "one-size-fits-all" regional innovation policy but a "one-size-fits-many" policy strategy. Indeed, RIAs will be most relevant in regional innovation systems that possess the following six conditions. First, the RIS has a distinct and proud regional culture. Second, the RIS has clear administrative boundaries. Third, the RIS has a city with a metropolitan population of at least around 1,000,000 inhabitants. The population is used here as a proxy to evaluate the potential sophistication of the RIS and innovative threshold for the RIS to compete globally. Fourth, the RIS has existing innovative infrastructures, such as universities, large companies, research centers, public institutions, and support and intermediary organizations. Fifth, the region has some political stability to fund the agency for a period of least 15 years. Finally, the region has a middle-income or high-income with a GDP per capita in the regional innovation system of at least USD $2,000-3,000. Moreover, the RIA will be most adequate in regions that are relatively specialized and that are organizationally and institutionally thick.

The Regional Innovation Agency. Ruta N Medellín is the outcome of a shared vision for regional economic development. The organization provides a best-practice model for regional development through science, technology, and innovation for many regions around the world. Due to its innovative institutional arrangement and unique governance structure, Ruta N has, however, experienced in its development many difficulties that have hindered the organization in efficiently and systematically transforming its RIS. Ruta N is a clear example of "policy running ahead of theory" that has followed more of an iterative path of trials-and-errors to define its role and mission in the RIS rather than a clear strategy. The following subsections provide a toolkit for policymakers to create their own version of a regional innovation agency in regions located on the knowledge periphery that can benefit from such an intervention (see previous section).

General Features. The creation of a regional innovation agency must be the outcome of a shared regional vision involving many different leading regional actors coming from public institutions, private companies, universities, and the civil society (quadruple helix). The number of regional actors must be wide enough to be representative of the regional innovation system. The actors should participate in defining the mission, vision, and overall strategy of the agency for the regional innovation system. Similar to an entrepreneurial discovery process in smart specialization strategy, the actors should define the priorities and participate in defining which new industrial path development to pursue. As a result, the shared regional vision should emerge from the co-creation process among the leading regional actors in the RIS.

The regional innovation agency should operate for a period of at least 15 years to significantly have an impact on its RIS. The RIA needs to be, as a result, relatively independent from political changes in the municipal, regional, or national governments. The RIA needs to be financially sustainable with steady streams of incomes coming from the government and other sources without being negatively affected by election results or external events. The agency also must be directly accountable to the civil society, and, as a public organization, to work for the common regional good and not for some vested economic or political interests or business elites. Without this quadruple helix support and widespread involvement in the process, the RIA may lack a coherent vision and sufficient cohesiveness to enable long-term performance.

The RIA's financing structure should come from multiple sources, namely from the municipal, regional, or national government, international development aid agencies, international and national agreements, and the RIA's own generated revenues. In regions experiencing significant regional corruptions and/or limited public capabilities, such as South Italy, the regional innovation agency can be conditionally funded through the European Regional Development Fund (ERDF) and operated by the national government or a supranational organization, such as the EU.

The employees working for the regional innovation agency need to possess the following qualities. First, they should have high academic qualifications in relevant majors at master or PhD levels. Second, they should have prior relevant professional and academic experience in leading innovation hubs around the world. Third, they should be passionate about their region and have an extensive understanding of the regional context. Fourth, they should be diverse with different professional and educational backgrounds in public policy, public affairs, entrepreneurship, science, innovation management, social psychology, and public management. Fifth, they should have the capacity to become knowledge gatekeepers by translating extra-regional knowledge to make it relevant to the local actors in the regional innovation system.

The RIA needs to work closely with a regional research organization in the creation of new programs, such as a regional institute for innovation. The regional institute for innovation should provide scientific evidence to support the RIA to make the best decisions for the RIS. The regional institute for innovation can be a research group from a regional university with the roles to monitor weaknesses in the RIS, to monitor international best-practices, to screen potential international actors with knowledge relevant for the RIS, to screen trends in emerging technologies, to screen trends in place-based and place-sensitive policies, to monitor trends in the academic literature on regional economic development, and to provide tools to evaluate the RIA. As a result, the regional institute works as an information-system for the RIA to pursue the most relevant strategic decisions. The regional institute for innovation has the role of gathering scientific evidence and thus working on more basic research, while the RIA has a more applied role.

Ruta N's undeniable achievement has been the creation of the Ruta N innovation center. The creation of an innovation center, such as the Ruta N Building Complex, has four main benefits. First, it anchors the RIA into the urban fabric and provides a science, technology, and innovation showcase for the RIA and the actors in the RIS. Second, it facilitates regional interactions between the agency and the startups, universities, research centers, and private companies located in the innovation centers, thus creating a sense of "local buzz" that continuously provides feedback to the agency on its actions. Third, it provides the RIA with a stable revenue stream from renting office and retail spaces. Fourth, the innovation center provides considerable media exposure from local and international media outlets. Fifth, the innovation center symbolizes the political commitment to science, technology, and innovation in the region, which is a concrete public benefit for the residents and provides confidence in the government to foreign investors.

Framework for Selecting New Industrial Path Development. One of the RIA's primary objectives is to support new industrial path development in the region. New industrial path development can be selected according to the concept of Entrepreneurial Discovery Process (EDP) of the Smart Specialization Strategy (S3), based on the framework developed by Balland, Boschma, Crespo, and Rigby (2017) (see Figure 3). The new industrial path development should be selected in the following manner. First, the selected technological trajectories must have high product complexity in order for the region to reach high benefits from pursuing the new industrial path development. Second, the ratio of low relatedness versus high relatedness has to be 1 to 3. Indeed, unrelated technological trajectories are risky since the region does not have prior capabilities and relies on extra-regional knowledge to build capabilities. Related technological trajectories that are more complex are less risky while offering high benefits to the region. Unrelated technological trajectories have to be selected where the product has the most links to other products following the product space theory (Hidalgo, Klinger, Barabási, & Hausmann, 2007). The role of the regional innovation agency is to support the selected sectors or subsectors to reach higher complexity through the recombination process between internal with external knowledge. Moreover, an observatory such as the STI Observatory should be created to generate a regional instrument for continuous Entrepreneurial Discovery Process since the paths selected are constantly evolving.

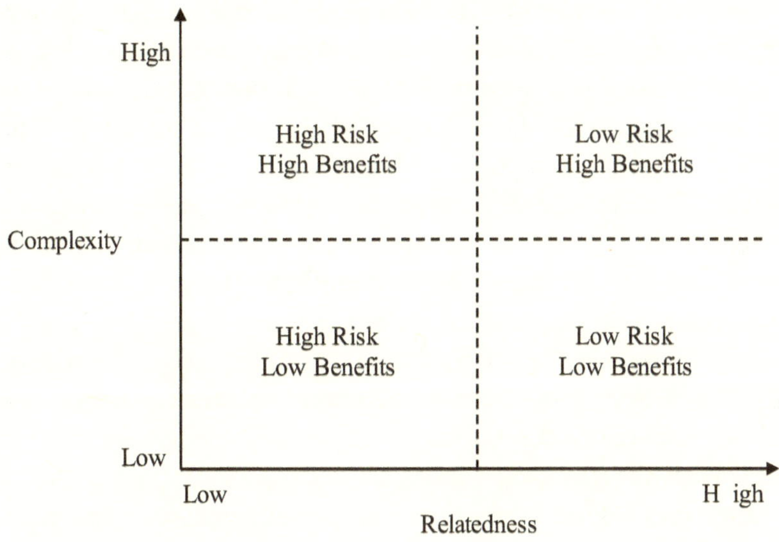

Figure 3. A Framework for Smart Specialization. Source: (Balland, Boschma, Crespo, & Rigby, 2017).

New industrial path development not only have to be selected according to the previous framework but also have to be the outcome of a common regional vision involving many different actors, coming from public institutions, private companies, universities, and the civil society. The selected new industrial path development need to stir passions and to bind together the actors in the RIS to the shared vision for the region. As a result, the selected new industrial path development can not only be the result of rigid data-driven and rational decision-making but also of a collective co-creation process that plays with the "animal spirit" and "regional aspirations" of the actors in the RIS. The regional innovation agencies can preselect a number of potential paths for the region that will be later discussed and selected by regional leaders in order to compromise between scientific data-driven decision-making and the regional's animal spirit

The Roles of the Regional Innovation Agency. The RIA should work as an intermediary organization in the RIS. More specifically, the

RIA should work as a knowledge gatekeeper that is not directly involved in implementing programs but rather has the following roles. First, the RIA should constantly screen successful innovation systems around the world. Second, the RIA should identify weaknesses in the actors of the RIS. Third, the RIA needs support local actors to acquire extra-regional knowledge. Fourth, the RIA needs play the role of a knowledge gatekeeper that supports the assimilation, or "tropicalization", of the relevant extra-regional knowledge into the RIS. The term "knowledge tropicalization" can be used for regions that are located between the tropics of Cancer and Capricorn. The process of tropicalization involves the RIA's assistance to the international actors implementing programs to contextualize the extra-regional knowledge to facilitate its absorption into the RIS. Fifth, the RIA should strengthen the region's socio-institutional structure to further facilitate the acquisition, assimilation, and exploitation of extra-regional knowledge in the RIS. Finally, the RIA should be a platform to facilitate regional and extra-regional interactions to create a sense of "local buzz" and to support the creation of regional and international networks

The RIA should also facilitate the co-evolution of the socio-institutional structure with the new industrial path development. Programs should affect the evolution of the regional social, organizational, and institutional structures by selecting socio-institutional changes in regions located at the technological frontier. In periods of structural change in the economy, the RIA must recouple the socio-institutional structure with the novel techno-economic structure to limit inefficiencies and instabilities resulting from structural change the regional economy. In addition, the RIA needs to accelerate the evolution of the socio-institutional structure to strengthen the local actors' capacity to acquire, to exploit, and to absorb extra-regional knowledge. The RIA's roles are significantly different from the role of the regional investment promotion agency that aims to attract international companies and Foreign Direct Investments (FDIs) into the RIS. Both regional innovation agency and regional investment promotion agency should, however, collaborate closely and follow a shared vision for the region.

Local Buzz and Global Pipelines. The RIA needs to foster interactions among regional actors and between regional and extra-regional actors. The RIA has to foster a sense of "local buzz," which refers to the information and communication ecology created by face-to-face contacts, co-presence and co-location of people and firms within the same industry and place or region, which thus facilitates the exchange of tacit knowledge (Storper & Venables, 2004). The regional sense of local buzz is thus achieved by promoting face-to-face interactions between different actors. The RIA needs to foster the creation of local networks, local events, and local initiatives that promote the sense of regional buzz. As a result, the RIA can promote regional networks connecting different actors in the RIS working towards specific technologies. Local events can range from networking events, conferences, monthly innovation lunches, to a weekly event dedicated to innovation. Regional initiatives should primarily promote repeated face-to-face interactions between private companies-universities-public institutions-civil society working towards specific technologies. The RIA can also promote regional interactions by creating an innovation center and/or an innovation district. The RIA promotes regional face-to-face interactions or the sense of "local buzz" to accelerate the diffusion of global pipelines and thus to foster the recombination process between extra-regional knowledge and regional knowledge.

The Organizational Structure of the Regional Innovation Agency. The regional innovation agency should be structured as follows: the board of directors should be headed by an elected official, from the municipal or regional government. The board should include funding partners, such as national government, when funds come from the national government, or supranational entity, when funds come from a development bank. If funds come from a public company, such as it is the case for Medellín, then the public company should be in the board. The board should include regional associations representing the business, cultural, civil society, and entrepreneurial interests—not only to bring more legitimacy to the agency but also to improve the RIA's capacity to rally and to reach key decision leaders. The board should include regional universities since they are the research and training instrument of any successful innovation system. Finally, the board should consist of diverse public-private organizations that work in innovation-related or research activities. The board of directors is responsible for setting priorities and strategic missions.

Support functions should include an executive director who is appointed by the board, and who directly oversees the marketing, communications, administration, and finance areas. Marketing and Communications have the role in promoting the agency and the innovation system in regional, national, and international media outlets, on social media, to sponsor regional events, to conduct communication campaigns, and to supervise the agency's websites. The Chief Operation Director works as a Project Management Office (PMO) overseeing the RIA's daily operations and is in charge of the RIA's evaluation. The Chief Strategy Director closely collaborates with the regional institute for innovation to screen, monitor, and find weaknesses in the RIS. The Chief Strategy Director sits in each quadruple helix committee. The Chief Strategy Director provides mentorship when designing new programs and supports working function directors in delivering programs. The Chief Strategy Director works in collaboration with the regional institute for innovation looking for new potential disruptive projects in the regional innovation system. The Chief Strategy Director also oversees consulting projects from outside organizations that aim to replicate the RIA's model or programs. The Chief Strategy Director directly oversees the working sub-function, disruptive projects. The Chief Strategy Director is also, with the Executive Director, the main representative of the RIA abroad.

Working functions should include four areas: social, organizational, institutional, science and technology. The social working function should adapt the social structure to changing economic paradigms through creating programs to adapt the culture, norms, values, and to diffuse the novel culture, norms, and values into the RIS. The organizational working function should support the development of internal processes facilitating the innovation process at the level of large companies, SMEs, and startups. The institutional working function should support public, public-private, and not-for-profit organizations that implement formal institutions to become more efficient and innovative in the new economic paradigm. The institutional working function supports the organizations that devise formal institutions with policy recommendations to promote science, technology, and innovation in the RIS. The science and technology working function aims to directly impact the scientific and technological capabilities as well as new industrial path development in the RIS. Furthermore, employees should be given the opportunity to rotate to other function areas every 18 months to facilitate the diffusion of knowledge within the organization.

Designing the Programs. Design of the programs should be the outcome of an institutional arrangement that involves all the most important actors in the RIS through multiple quadruple helices. The RIA must monitor the weaknesses in the RIS through gathering primary data from all the most important actors in the RIS. The weaknesses in the RIS are identified by the regional institute for innovation, the internal monitoring of best-practices conducted by the Chief Strategy Director, and the quadruple helix advisory boards in each working function and working sub-function. Each quadruple helix advisory board should include at least 10 different actors who are performing significant activities in the working function and in the working sub-function. Each quadruple helix advisory board has to meet four times a year. In the quadruple helix advisory boards at the level of working functions, the advisory boards will be responsible for deliberating on a plan of action to respond to the priorities set by the board of directors. In the quadruple helix advisory boards at the level of working sub-functions, the advisory board will be responsible for defining the programs to address the lines in the plan of action. The quadruple helix advisory boards should be as diverse as possible while being adapted to the context of the RIS.

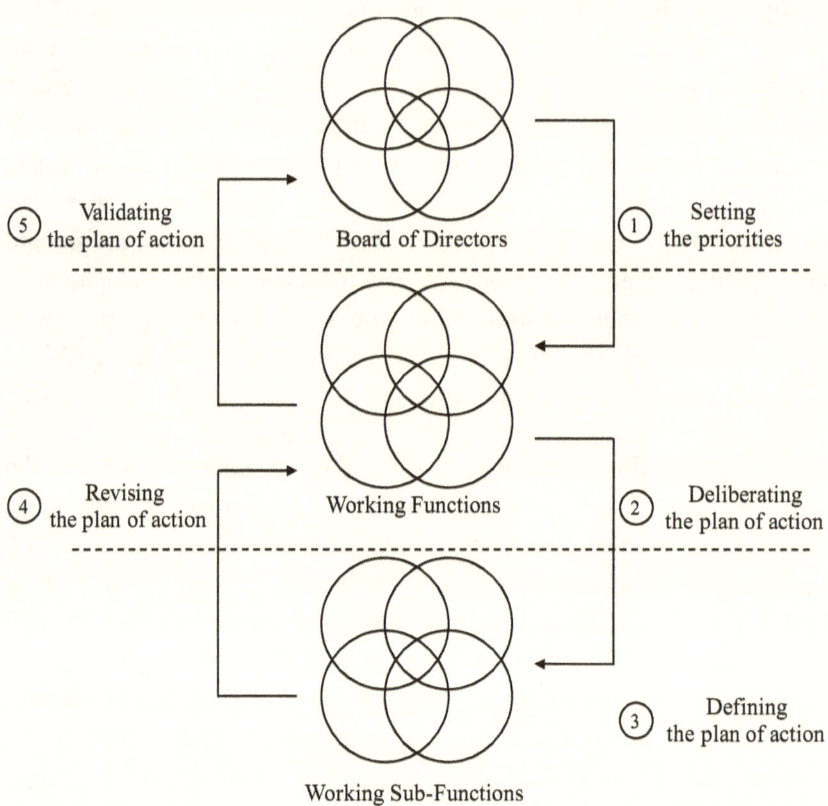

Figure 4. Institutional Arrangements for Designing New Programs.
Source: own design.

The Programs. The regional innovation agency's vocation is not to implement programs but rather to support other actors in the RIS to identify, to design, to implement, and to monitor programs that address relevant weaknesses in the RIS. In rare cases, however, when the RIA identifies a weakness in the RIS that can be addressed with a short-term program and cannot be implemented by an existing regional or extra-regional actor, the RIA can create and implement a pilot program by benchmarking international best-practices in collaboration with the regional institute for innovation.

Evaluating the Regional Innovation Agency. The RIA should be evaluated in a formative and summative manner. The RIA will operate for at least 15 years, and so needs to continuously evolve to respond to the needs emerging in the RIS. Formative evaluation will be performed to improve the trajectory of the organization in an incremental manner, while the summative evaluation will allow for new dynamics and more radical approaches to emerge. The RIA should evaluate its impact on three different levels. Indeed, RIA should monitor its impact at the RIS level, at the agency level, and at the programs level. The evaluations should take into account that the RIA ultimately has a limited impact on the RIS, a moderate impact on the agency, and a high impact on the programs.

Conclusions.

As any other conceptual tool, *The Entrepreneurial Region* is not the panacea for regional economic development, but it provides some interesting policy concepts for policymakers to experiment with. Ultimately, the success of its implementation depends on regional actors' capabilities, willingness, and legitimacy to carry out regional economic development and structural change. In many countries, it will require national governments to devolve additional powers to regional governments to design and implement their Science, Technology, and Innovation Plans and support them to act more entrepreneurially. *The Entrepreneurial Region* provides some answers to two of the shortcomings of *The Entrepreneurial State*. First, *The Entrepreneurial Region* points out that regions in the Global South lacking institutional, financial, and/or technological capabilities still have a role to play in the innovation process. Second, *The Entrepreneurial Region* argues that regions must promote knowledge diffusion and absorptive capacity to accelerate the technological catch-up process.

Regions in the Global South often lack the institutional, financial, and/or technological capabilities to foster new regional technological trajectories, and thus promote the technological catching-up process. Due to their entrepreneurial nature, regional innovation agencies (RIAs) have the flexibility, the independence from political influences, the managerial autonomy—particularly regarding personnel and financial management—and the institutional capabilities that can surrogate a weak regional innovation system in order to strengthen it. Financial stability from political influences is important to achieve, as a political decision could jeopardize the existence of the agency, such as the infamous case of the regional development agencies in the United Kingdom (Pike et al., 2018). Due to their flexibility and legitimacy to design and implement place-based policies, regional innovation agencies have more leeway to break evolutionary mechanisms and promote regional economic development than traditional intermediary organizations. Indeed, due to their institutional arrangements involving multiple stakeholders coming from the public sector, the private sector, academia, and the civil society, regional innovation agencies can rally a wide range of regional stakeholders with different interests around a common regional vision. Moreover, regional innovation agencies provide some stability to promote long-term innovation policy strategies and the design and implementation of place-based policies more freely from political influences and electoral results.

Regional policymakers often overestimate their regional innovation systems' capacity to develop new ideas and to produce technological innovations. Regional innovation policies would often be more efficient in promoting the local's absorptive capacity and in adapting to their context's existing innovations. One of the main activities regional innovation agencies perform is to monitor, acquire, assimilate, and diffuse extra-regional knowledge. The regional technological catch-up process is achieved by responding to regional weaknesses. Regional innovation agencies must actively engage quadruple helix stakeholders at each step of the policy design, implementation, and evaluation if they are to correctly identify the weaknesses in the RIS and the extra-regional actors best placed to address those weaknesses. In contrast to smart specialization strategy (S3), which argues that regions must discover what they do best in terms of their scientific and technological endowments, this book argues that regional weaknesses must be the starting point of policy action. Another main activity of regional innovation agencies is to manage and oversee multiple quadruple helix advisory boards, involving the most important regional actors in science and technology, and in the social, organizational, and institutional structure.

The Entrepreneurial Region recommends creating regional innovation agencies (RIAs) in metropolitan-regions to design and support the implementation of place-based policies. The regional innovation agency's vocation is not to implement programs, but rather to support other actors in the RIS to identify, to design, to implement, and to monitor programs that address relevant weaknesses in the RIS. This policy recommendation fits particularly well metropolitan-regions on the knowledge periphery and with relatively large innovative infrastructures (universities, large companies, research centers, public institutions, and support and intermediary organizations). The policy recommendation to create regional innovation agencies in regions on the knowledge periphery is not a silver bullet. Safeguards should be put in place to avoid rent-seeking and policy capturing from powerful vested economic interests that could ultimately lead to a situation of political lock-in. The safeguards could be, for instance, to have an oversight from the civil society, through co-creation web-platforms and national or supranational authorities.

From the 1970s to 2000s, Medellín was isolated from global knowledge flows due to a period of extreme violence, as well as due to idiosyncratic cultural, social, and geographical factors. This isolation contributed to the cognitive and political lock-ins of the industrial sector, which hindered the city's transformation into a more knowledge-based economy. The limited diffusion of extra-regional knowledge contributed to system failures, which required some policy interventions. At the center of Medellín's transformation is the *Grupo Empresarial Antioqueño,* which acted as institutional entrepreneurs to influence policy interventions. The GEA was motivated to act as institutional entrepreneurs to reinforce their leaderships in the region's political economy, to capture policies to support its restructure towards more knowledge-based activities, to limit instabilities from regional structural change—learning from past regional structural changes in the 1980s that led to worst economic and social period in Medellín's history, to limit the influence of competing elite groups such as "narco-elites", and to promote regional economic development from their paternalistic regional vision.

Mayor Fajardo (2004-2007), Alonso Salazar (2008-2011), and Aníbal Gaviria (2012-2015), who were backed by the GEA, have led to structural reforms in education, social urbanism, social inclusion, and innovation-led policies, paving the way for Medellín's economic transformation into a more knowledge-based and service-based city. The institutional proximity and shared vision between the private sector, namely, the GEA and Proantioquia, and the public sector, namely, the City of Medellín and EPM-UNE, has facilitated the creation of an institutional instrument, that is Ruta N, to connect Medellín to innovation hubs around the world and to accelerate Medellín's transformation into a knowledge city. The regional innovation agency emerged from the proximity between the municipal government under the leadership of Alonso Salazar (2008-2011) and the GEA under the leadership of Nicanor Restrepo Santamaría (1978-2015). The institutional proximity between the local government and the GEA emerged from the paternalistic sense that traditionally possesses the Antioquian elites towards regional economic and social development.

The Entrepreneurial Region can support new industrial path development through the acquisition, diffusion, and absorption of extra-regional knowledge in regions located on the knowledge periphery. In Medellín, Ruta N has played the role of a knowledge gatekeeper that has "tropicalized" extra-regional knowledge to facilitate its absorption into the RIS. The act of tropicalizing knowledge, which refers to the hybridization of the tacit extra-regional knowledge with local knowledge, aims to facilitate regional absorptive capacity. The knowledge gatekeeper is in charge of supporting new industrial regional path development by connecting local actors with international leaders while monitoring and facilitating knowledge transfer. In contrast with other knowledge gatekeepers, such as leader firms or universities, in which a lag persists in leaking knowledge, the extra-regional knowledge from public knowledge gatekeepers is directly transferred to the actors in the RIS. The public knowledge gatekeeper, Ruta N, has three roles: to support the acquisition of extra-regional knowledge, its "tropicalization," and its diffusion into the RIS. For the RIA, the brokerage of extra-regional knowledge has three objectives: first, to improve the capacity of the RIS to acquire, absorb, and diffuse extra-regional knowledge; second, to connect Medellín and Ruta N to significant innovation hubs around the world, such as Boston,

Austin, Silicon Valley, Israel, or Cambridge, to generate formal and informal networks between regional and international actors; and third, to improve the visibility of Medellín and Ruta N as an important innovation system in the world. Ultimately, regional innovation agencies in regions on the knowledge periphery should reorient their strategies after having successfully supported their regions' transformation into more knowledge-based activities.

"If you were asking me what the role of Ruta N should be, I would answer that Ruta N's role is to coordinate and to create the conditions for innovation. Let me put it to you that way, if Ruta N were to be successful, it should cease to exist" (personal communication, 19 July 2017).

The creation of new industrial path development is not done in a vacuum since it affects and is affected by the socio-institutional structure, which is a path-dependent and evolutionary structure. The academic literature has pointed out the importance of socio-institutional changes to facilitate technology transfer and new industrial path development (See Perez, 2010). The socio-institutional structure suffers from inertia, and thus co-evolves less rapidly than technological change during periods of structural change in the economy characterized by rapid path creation and path destruction. In regions located on the knowledge periphery, the coupling of the socio-institutional structure with the techno-economic structure must be facilitated by the entrepreneurial region. Indeed, contrary to core regions at the technological frontier that experience trials and errors when dealing with recoupling their socio-institutional structures with the new technological paradigm, regions on the knowledge periphery that are catching-up can learn from the errors of core regions by selecting the traits that are most important for an efficient coupling.

In Medellín, Ruta N has created programs to accelerate the evolution of social, organizational, and institutional structures. The social structure was affected by increasing innovative attitudes, entrepreneurial spirit, and

STEM career aspirations among residents. The organizational structure was affected by transforming existing private large companies and SMEs into entrepreneurial entities that are continuously innovating. The organizational structure was affected by providing employees' training in innovation management and transference of methodologies to foster innovations. The institutional structure was affected by creating programs targeting local institutions, namely the City of Medellín, educational institutions, linkage institutions, and technological research centers. Finally, Ruta N is building an innovation district as a high-quality urban space, which clusters innovative actors to promote face-to-face interactions and to speed up the exchange of tacit knowledge. The dimension of geographic proximity is an enabler of the socio-institutional structure, since it facilitates repeated and frequent interactions—and thus the exchange of tacit knowledge contributing to the adoption and diffusion of new knowledge. Finally, the socio-institutional structures affect each other through feedback loops and cumulative causation mechanisms. As a result, the social, organizational, or institutional structures cannot fully co-evolve without the concurrent co-evolution of the other two.

From the case of Ruta N and Medellín, this book derives three main policy recommendations for *The Entrepreneurial Region*. First, regional policymakers should empower regional business elites to act as institutional entrepreneurs and encourage the alignment of interests between regional political and business elites. In contrast to transnational elites, or place-less actors, people or organizations "who are not expected to care about the consequences of their decisions for particular places and communities" (Hambleton, 2015, p. 167), regional business elites—like the GEA—in second-tier cities have place-based vested interests, a strong sense of regional pride, and have thus a stronger incentive to participate in regional economic development. Second, regional innovation agencies can be powerful entrepreneurial instruments to design and support the implementation of place-based policies since it can rally diverse regional actors around a common regional vision. Third, regions, especially peripheral regions and those on the knowledge periphery, must contextualize, "tropicalize", international best-practices. The recombination between international best-practices and the local contexts can generate the most effective place-based policies. Ultimately, extra-regional policy best-practices can facilitate the design and implementation of place-based and place-sensitive policies in regions on the knowledge periphery that might lack the institutional capacities to create their place-based policies from scratch.

There are, of course, many cases of regions besides Medellín that have started to act more entrepreneurially. The United States have generated many interesting cases where the local and regional governments are acting entrepreneurially thanks to specific institutional contexts, an active community mindset from the regional business elites, and bottom-up associations to stir regional transformation. In Boston, the Mayor's Office has created the department of New Urban Mechanics to experiment with new approaches to government and civic life. The department has controversially popularized micro-units—apartments of 385-square-feet or 36-square-meters—to curb the housing crisis in Boston (City of Boston, 2018). In Chattanooga, the Mayor's Office, the municipally-owned utility company, EPB, and place-based foundations have been able to reverse the decline of the city. The Enterprise Center, a public-private partnership, was created to support the development of Chattanooga's innovation district. The Enterprise Center is an institutional arrangement that gives the City of Chattanooga and real-estate developers more flexibility in designing and implementing innovation with social policies to limit social problems when pursuing the creation of an innovation district (Morisson & Bevilacqua, 2018). The European Commission requires regions to develop a Smart Specialization Strategy (S3) to access European Cohesion Funds. S3 is a policy concept to support regional prioritization in innovative sectors, fields, or technologies through the entrepreneurial discovery process, a bottom-up approach to reveal what a region does best in terms of its endowments in science and technology (Foray, David, & Hall, 2009). Despite many design and implementation challenges for many regions, it has increased the awareness of the strategic importance of regions in the innovation process (Foray, 2018; Marques & Morgan, 2018). In China, the ambitious policy strategy in Artificial Intelligence with the Artificial Intelligence Development Plan devolves some power to regions to devise policy strategies and to experiment with policies (The State Council, 2017).

This book aims to convey a positive message for regions around the world, illustrating with the case of Medellín that many regions can transform themselves into entrepreneurial regions as well. As an analogy for *The Entrepreneurial Region* (as used in Dixit, 2009), imagine you were preparing for an expedition to the South Pole. Would you rather prepare like Roald Amundsen or Robert Scott? The two explorers were in a race to set the first foot on the South Pole in 1911. Amundsen combined some knowledge from the Netsilik Eskimos—learning to dog-sled, using leather and fur clothing, and bringing with him Greenlander huskies—with Western technologies, while contextualizing that knowledge living in his base camp in Antarctica. Scott relied on the latest Western technologies, most notably British, since they were the best (undoubtedly). The end game was quite different. Amundsen won the race and Scott and his entire team perished without ever reaching the South Pole. *The Entrepreneurial Region* should be like Amundsen in that it should be critical enough to know its weaknesses, independent enough to find the best solutions, smart enough to contextualize those solutions to address its weaknesses, and flexible enough to rally the most important regional stakeholders around a common inclusive and sustainable vision.

References.

Abramovitz, M. (1956). Resource and Output Trends in the United States since 1870. In *Resource and output trends in the United States since 1870* (pp. 1-23). Cambridge, MA: National Bureau of Economic Research.

Acemoglu, D. & Autor, D. (2011) Skills, Tasks and Technologies: Implications for Employment and Earnings. *Handbook of Labor Economics, 4*, 1043–1171.

Aghion, P., & Howitt, P. (1990). *A Model of Growth Through Creative Destruction.* Working Paper No. 3223. Cambridge, MA: National Bureau of Economic Research.

Akcigit, U., Grigsby, J., & Nicholas, T. (2017). *The Rise of American Ingenuity: Innovation and Inventors of the Golden Age.* Working Paper No. 23047. Cambridge, MA: National Bureau of Economic Research.

Alcaldía de Medellín & Banco Interamericano de Desarrollo (2009). *Medellín: Transformación de una Ciudad.* Medellín: Alcaldía de Medellín.

Alcaldía de Medellín. (2007). *Del Miedo a la Esperanza.* Medellín: Alcaldía de Medellín.

Alcaldía de Medellín. (2008). *Plan de Desarrollo 2008-2011. Medellín ES Solidaria y Competitiva.* Medellín: Alcaldía de Medellín.

Alcaldía de Medellín. (2012). *Medellín, Modelo de Transformación Urbana. Proyecto Urbano Integral Nororiental y Consolidación Habitacional en la Quebrada Juan Bobo.* Medellín: Alcaldía de Medellín.

Allen, T. J. (1977). *Managing the Flow of Technology: Technology Transfer and the Dissemination of Technological Information within the R&D Organization.* Cambridge: MIT Press.

Almirall, E., Wareham, J., Ratti, C., Conesa, P., Bria, F., Gaviria, A., & Edmondson, A. (2016). Smart Cities at the Crossroads: New Tensions in City Transformation. *California Management Review, 59*(1), 141-152.

Alvarez, V. (1996). Poblamiento y Poblacion en el Valle de Aburra y Medellín 1541-1951. In Melo, J. O. (Eds.). *Historia de Medellín: Tomo I* (pp. 57-84). Bogotá: Compañía Suramericana de Seguros.

Amable, B. (1993). Catch-up and Convergence: A Model of Cumulative Growth. *International Review of Applied Economics, 7*(1), 1-25.

Amin, A. (1994). *Post-Fordism: A Reader*. Oxford: Blackwell.

Amnesty International. (2005). *The Paramilitaries in Medellín: Demobilization or Legalization?*. London: Amnesty International.

Amsden, A. (1989). *Asia's Next Giant: South Korea and Late Industrialization*. Oxford: Oxford University Press.

Arias Trujillo, J. R. (2011). *Historia de Colombia Contemporánea (1920-2010)*. Bogotá: Universidad de los Andes.

Arthur, W. B. (1988). Self-reinforcing Mechanisms in Economies. In Anderson, R. W., Arrow, K. J., & and Pines, D. (Eds.). *The Economy as an Evolving Complex System* (pp. 9-33). Redwood City, CA: Addison-Wesley.

Arthur, W. B. (1996). Increasing Returns and the Two Worlds of Business. *Harvard Business Review, 74*(4), 100-109.

Asheim, B., & Gertler, M. (2004). Understanding Regional Innovation Systems. In Fagerberg, J., Mowery, D. & Nelson, R. R. (Eds). *Handbook of Innovation*. Oxford: Oxford University Press.

Ashoka. (2014). The Transformation of Medellín, and the Surprising Company Behind it. *Forbes*, January, 24, 2014. Retrieved from https://www.forbes.com/sites/ashoka/2014/01/27/the-transformation-of-Medellín-and-the-surprising-company-behind-it/#61d42aa4232c

Audretsch, D. B., & Feldman, M. P. (1996). Innovative clusters and the industry life cycle. *Review of industrial organization, 11*(2), 253-273.

Autor, D. (2014). *Polanyi's Paradox and the Shape of Employment Growth*. Working Paper No. 20485. Cambridge, MA: National Bureau of Economic Research.

Avilés, W. (2006). Paramilitarism and Colombia's Low-Intensity Democracy. *Journal of Latin American Studies, 38(2), 379-408.*

Ayres, R. U. (2006). Turning point: The end of exponential growth?. *Technological Forecasting and Social Change, 73*(9), 1188-1203.

Bagnasco, A. (1977). *Tre Italie: La Problematica Territoriale dello Sviluppo.* Bologna: Il Mulino

Balland, P.-A., Boschma, R., Crespo, J., & Rigby, D. (2017). *Smart Specialization Policy in the EU: Relatedness, Knowledge Complexity and Regional Diversification* (Papers in Evolutionary Economic Geography No. 17.17). Utrecht: Utrecht University.

Barca, F. (2009). *An Agenda for A Reformed Cohesion Policy: A Place-Based Approach to Meeting European Union Challenges and Expectations.* Independent Report. Brussels: European Commission.

Barca, F., McCann, P., & Rodríguez-Pose, A. (2012). The case for regional development intervention: place-based versus place-neutral approaches. *Journal of regional science, 52*(1), 134-152.

Barro, R. J., & Sala-i-Martin, X. (1992). Convergence. *Journal of political Economy, 100*(2), 223-251.

Bateman, M., Duran Ortíz, J-P. & Maclean, K. (2010). *A post-Washington consensus approach to local economic development in Latin America? An example from Medellín, Colombia.* (Background Note, April 2011), London: Overseas Development Institute (ODI).

Bathelt, H., Malmberg, A., & Maskell, P. (2004). Clusters and Knowledge: Local Buzz, Global Pipelines and the Process of Knowledge Creation. *Progress in Human Geography, 28*(1), 31-56.

Bator, F. M. (1958). The Anatomy of Market Failure. *The Quarterly Journal of Economics, 72*(3), 351-379.

Baumol, W. J. (1996). Entrepreneurship: Productive, Unproductive, and Destructive. *Journal of Business Venturing, 11*(1), 3-22.

BBC. (2010). Elton John Naples gig gets organisers into hot water. Retrieved from https://www.bbc.com/news/world-europe-11798788

Beaudry, P., Green, D. A. & Sand, B. M. (2013). *The Great Reversal in the Demand for Skill and Cognitive Tasks*. Cambridge, MA: National Bureau of Economic Research.

Belussi, F., & Sedita, S. R. (2010). Localized and Distance Learning in Industrial Districts. In Belussi, F. & Sammarra, A. (Eds). *Business Networks in Clusters and Industrial Districts. The Governance of the Global Value Chain* (pp. 24-51). Abingdon: Routledge.

Bergquist, K., Fink, C., & Raffo, J. (2017). *Identifying and ranking the world's largest clusters of inventive activity*, WIPO Economic Research Paper No. 37, WIPO: Geneva.

Bértola, L., & Ocampo, J. A. (2012). *The Economic Development of Latin America since Independence*. New York: Oxford University Press.

Boschma, R. (2005). Proximity and Innovation: A Critical Assessment. *Regional Studies, 39*(1), 61-74.

Boschma, R. A., & Frenken, K. (2006). Why is Economic Geography not an Evolutionary Science? Towards an Evolutionary Economic Geography. *Journal of Economic Geography, 6*(3), 273-302.

Boschma, R., & Lambooy, J. G. (1999). Evolutionary Economics and Economic Geography. *Journal of Evolutionary Economics, 9*(4), 411-429.

Boschma, R., & Van der Knaap, G. A. (1997). New Technology and Windows of Locational Opportunity: Indeterminacy, Creativity and Chance. In Reijnders, J. (Eds.). *Economics and Evolution (pp. 171-202)*. Cheltenham: Edward Elgar.

Boschma, R., Minondo, A., & Navarro, M. (2013). The emergence of new industries at the regional level in Spain: a proximity approach based on product relatedness. *Economic Geography, 89*(1), 29-51.

Botero Herrera, F. (1996). *Medellín 1890-1950: Historia Urbana y Juego de Intereses*. Medellín: Editorial Universidad de Antioquia,

Brodzinsky, S. (2014). From murder capital to model city: is Medellín's miracle show or substance?. *The Guardian*. Retrieved from http://www.theguardian.com/cities/2014/apr/17/Medellín-murder-capital-to-model-city-miracle-un-world-urban-forum

Brynjolfsson, E., & McAfee, A. (2014). *The second machine age: Work, progress, and prosperity in a time of brilliant technologies*. New York: WW Norton & Company.

Caballero Argáez, C. (2016). *La Economía Colombiana del Siglo XX: Un Recorrido por la Historia y sus Protagonistas*. Bogotá: Penguin Random House.

Cairncross, F. (1997). *The Death of Distance*. Cambridge. MA: Harvard Business School Press.

Calle, C. (2015). Nicanor Restrepo: El Cerebro del GEA. *Proantioquia*. 18 March 2015. Retrieved from http://www.proantioquia.org.co/nicanor-restrepo-el-cerebro-del-sindicato-antioqueno/

Camagni, R. (1991). *Innovation Networks*. London: Belhaven Press.

Cameron, G. (1996). *Innovation and Economic Growth*. Centre for Economic Performance. London: London School of Economics and Political Science.

Caracol Radio Medellín. (2017). ¿Manos criminales en el presupuesto participativo de Medellín? *Caracol Radio Medellín*. Retrieved from http://caracol.com.co/emisora/2017/02/20/Medellín/1487616843_493366.html

Carlino, G. A. (1982). Manufacturing agglomeration economies as returns to scale: a production function approach. *Papers in Regional Science*, *50*(1), 95-108.

Castells, M. (1994). *The Informational City: Information Technology, Economic Structuring, and the Urban-Regional Process*. Oxford: Blackwell Publishing.

Castells, M. (1996). *The Rise of the Network Society*. Oxford: Blackwell Publishers.

Chang, H. J. (2011). Industrial policy: can we go beyond an unproductive confrontation?. In *Annual World Bank Conference on Development Economics* (pp. 83-109).

Charron, N., Dijkstra, L., & Lapuente, V. (2014). Regional governance matters: quality of government within European Union member states. *Regional Studies, 48*(1), 68-90.

Chittum, S. (2018). *Last Days of the Concorde: The Crash of Flight 4590 and the End of the Supersonic Passenger Travel.* Washington: Smithsonian Books.

City of Boston. (2018). Compact Living Pilot. Retrieved from https://www.boston.gov/departments/new-urban-mechanics/housing-innovation-lab/compact-living

City of Medellín. (2018). Indicadores y Estadísticas de Planeación. Retrieved from https://www.Medellín.gov.co/irj/portal/Medellín?NavigationTarget=navurl://ecd9e39fad34752203a60e8a84a34ba1

Cohen, W. M., & Levinthal, D. A. (1989). Innovation and Learning: The Two Faces of R&D. *The Economic Journal, 99*(397), 569-596.

Cohen, W. M., & Levinthal, D. A. (1990). Absorptive capacity: A new perspective on learning and innovation. *Administrative science quarterly, 35*(1), 128-152.

Concejo de Medellín. (2012). *Acuerdo Municipal 024 de 2012: Mediante el cual se Adopta el Plan de Ciencia, Tecnología e Innovación de Medellín.* Medellín: Concejo de Medellín.

Cowan, R., David, P. A., & Foray, D. (2000). The Explicit Economics of Knowledge Codification and Tacitness. *Industrial and corporate change, 9*(2), 211-253.

Dahlman, C. J. & Nelson, R. (1995). Social Absorption Capability, National Innovation Systems and Economic Development. In Perkins, H. D. & Koo, B. H. (Eds). *Social Capability and Long-Term Economic Growth* (pp. 82-122). London: Macmillan Press.

Dal Bó, E. (2006). Regulatory Capture: A Review. *Oxford Review of Economic Policy, 22*(2), 203-225.

DANE GEIH. (2018). Gran encuesta ntegrada de Hogares – GEIH – Mercado laboral históricos. Retrieved from https://www.dane.gov.co/index.php/estadisticas-por-tema/mercado-laboral/empleo-y-desempleo/geih-historicos.

DANE. (2018). Cuenta Departamentales. Retrieved from https://www.dane.gov.co/index.php/estadisticas-por-tema/cuentas-nacionales/cuentas-nacionales-departamentales

David, P. A. (1985). Clio and the Economics of QWERTY. *The American Economic Review, 75*(2), 332-337.

Deming, D. J. (2015). *The Growing Importance of Social Skills in the Labor Market.* Working Paper No. 21473. Cambridge: National Bureau of Economic Research.

Dinero. (2009). Lista la internacionalización de EPM. Retrieved from https://www.dinero.com/negocios/articulo/lista-internacionalizacion-epm/79894

Dixit, A. K. (2009). Governance Institutions and Economic Activity. *The American Economic Review, 99*(1), 3-24.

Dixit, A., K. (1996). *The Making of Economic Policy: A Transaction-Cost Perspective.* Cambridge: MIT Press.

Djankov, S., La Porta, R., Lopez-de-Silanes, F., & Shleifer, A. (2002). The Regulation of Entry. *Quarterly journal of Economics, 117*(1), 1-37.

Doloreux, D. (2003). Regional Innovation Systems in the Periphery: The Case of the Beauce in Québec (Canada). *International Journal of Innovation Management, 7*(01), 67-94.

Dosi, G. (1982). Technological Paradigms and Technological Trajectories: A Suggested Interpretation of the Determinants and Directions of Technical Change. *Research Policy, 11*(3), 147-162.

Dosi, G. (1988). Sources, Procedures, and Microeconomic Effects of Innovation. *Journal of Economic Literature, 26*, 1120-1171.

Dosi, G., Llerena, P., & Labini, M. S. (2006). The Relationships Between Science, Technologies and their Industrial Exploitation: An Illustration through the Myths and Realities of the so-called 'European Paradox'. *Research Policy, 35*(10), 1450-1464.

Douglas, P. C., & Cobb, C. W. (1928). A theory of production. *The American Economic Review, 18*(1), 139-165.

Drucker, P. F. (1994). *Post-capitalist Society*. Abingdon: Routledge.

Echeverri, A. & Orsini, F. (2010). Informalidad y Urbanismo Social en Medellín. In Hermelin, M, Echeverri, A., & Giraldo, J. (Eds.). *Medellín: Medio Ambiente, Urbanismo y Sociedad* (pp. 130-152). Medellín: Universidad EAFIT.

Edquist, C., & Johnson, B. (1997). Institutions and Organizations in Systems of Innovation. In Edquist, C. (Eds). *Systems of Innovation: Technologies, Institutions, and Organizations* (pp. 41-63). London: Routledge.

European Commision. (2018). New Cohesion Policy. Retrieved from http://ec.europa.eu/regional_policy/en/2021_2027/

European Commission. (2016). What are Technology Readiness Levels (TRLs) and to which Horizon 2020 call topics are they applicable? Retrieved from https://ec.europa.eu/research/participants/portal/desktop/en/support/faqs/fa q-2890.html

European Commission. (2018a). Available budget 2014-2020. Retrieved from http://ec.europa.eu/regional_policy/en/funding/available-budget/

European Commission. (2018b). R&D expenditures. Retrieved from https://ec.europa.eu/eurostat/statistics-explained/index.php/R_%26_D_expenditure

European Parliament. (2000). Lisbon European Council 23 and 24 March 2000. Presidency Conclusion. European Union. Retrieved from http://www.europarl.europa.eu/summits/lis1_en.htm

Fajardo Valderrama, S. (2007) *Medellín: La mas educada*. Medellín: Alcaldía de Medellín.

Fajardo, A., & Andrews, M. (2014). *Does successful governance require heroes? The case of Sergio Fajardo and the city of Medellín: A reform case for instruction* (No. 2014/035). WIDER Working Paper.

Farole, T., Rodriguez-Pose, A., & Storper, M. (2011). Human geography and the institutions that underlie economic growth. *Progress in Human Geography*, *35*(1), 58-80.

Filippone, R. (1994). The Medellín Cartel: Why we can't win the drug war. *Studies in Conflict & Terrorism*, *17*(4), 323-344.

Flanagan, K., & Uyarra, E. (2016). Four dangers in innovation policy studies – And how to avoid them. *Industry and Innovation*, *23*(2), 177–188.

Flanagan, K., Uyarra, E., & Laranja, M. (2011). Reconceptualising the 'policy mix' for innovation. *Research Policy*, *40*(5), 702-713.

Flikkema, M., De Man, A. P., & Castaldi, C. (2014). Are trademark counts a valid indicator of innovation? Results of an in-depth study of new Benelux trademarks filed by SMEs. *Industry and Innovation*, *21*(4), 310-331.

Florida, R. (2017). *The new urban crisis: How our cities are increasing inequality, deepening segregation, and failing the middle class—And what we can do about it*. New York: Basic Books.

Foray, D. (2018). Smart specialisation strategies and industrial modernisation in European regions—theory and practice. *Cambridge Journal of Economics*, *42*(6), 1505-1520.

Foray, D., David, P., & Hall, B. H. (2009). *Smart Specialisation – The Concept. Knowledge Economists*. Policy Brief Number 9, June. Brussels: European Commission, DG research.

Franco Restrepo, V. L. (2006). *Poder Regional y Proyecto Hegemónico: El Caso de la Ciudad Metropolitana de Medellín y su Entorno Regional, 1970-2000*. Medellín: Instituto Popular de Capacitación.

Franz, T. (2017). Urban Governance and Economic Development in Medellín: An "Urban Miracle"?. *Latin American Perspectives*, *44*(2), 52-70.

Franz, T. (2018). Power balances, transnational elites, and local economic governance: The political economy of development in Medellín. *Local Economy*, *33*(1), 85-109.

Freeland, C. (2012). *Plutocrats: The rise of the new global super-rich and the fall of everyone else*. London: Penguin.

Freeman, C. (1987). *Technology Policy and Economic Performance: Lessons from Japan*. London: Pinter.

Freeman, C. (1995). The 'National System of Innovation' in Historical Perspective. *Cambridge Journal of Economics, 19*(1), 5-24.

Freeman, C., & Soete, L. (2004). *The Economics of Industrial Innovation*. London: Thomson.

Frey, C. B., & Osborne, M. A. (2017). The Future of Employment: How Susceptible are Jobs to Computerisation?. *Technological Forecasting and Social Change, 114*, 254-280.

Friedman, T. L. (2005). *The World is Flat: A Brief History of the Twenty-First Century*. London: Macmillan.

Friedrichs, J. (1993). A theory of urban decline: economy, demography and political elites. *Urban Studies, 30*(6), 907-917.

Fuller, T. (2018). Life on the Dirtiest Block in San Francisco. *New York Times*. Retrieved from https://www.nytimes.com/2018/10/08/us/san-francisco-dirtiest-street-london-breed.html?module=inline

Gaceta Oficial N°3730. (2010). *Acuerdo Municipal N°49 DE 2010*. Medellín: Concejo de Medellín.

García Estrada, R. (1999). *Sociedad de Mejoras Públicas de Medellín: Cien Años Haciendo Ciudad*. Medellín: Sociedad de Mejoras Públicas.

Gertler, M. S. (2003). Tacit Knowledge and the Economic Geography of Context, or the Undefinable Tacitness of Being (There). *Journal of Economic Geography, 3*(1), 75-99.

Ghosh, S. & Nanda, N. (2010). Venture Capital Investment in the Clean Energy Sector. Harvard Business School Working Paper, 11=020. Retrieved from http://www.hbs.edu/faculty/Publication%20Files/11-020.pdf

Gibbons, J. F. (2000). The Role of Stanford University: A Dean's Reflections. In Lee, C. M. (Eds.). *The Silicon Valley edge: A habitat for innovation and entrepreneurship* (pp. 200-217). Stanford: Stanford University Press.

Gilly, J. P., & Torre, A. (2000). *Dynamiques de proximité*. Paris: Editions L'Harmattan.

Gómez, D. F., Aparicio, S., & Urbano, D. (2015). Capital Emprendedor y su Influencia sobre el Crecimiento Económico de Antioquia. In Gómez, D. F. (Eds.). *Una Apuesta por Medellín (pp. 17-39)*. Medellín: Corporación Universitaria Remington.

González Escobar, L. F. (2007). *Medellín, los orígenes y la transición a la modernidad: crecimiento y modelos urbanos 1775-1932*. Medellín: Escuela del Hábitat-CEHAP Universidad Nacional de Colombia Sede Medellín.

Goodman, L. S., & Mayer, C. (2018). Homeownership and the American Dream. *Journal of Economic Perspectives, 32*(1), 31-58.

Gordon, R. J. (2012). *Is US Economic Growth Over? Faltering Innovation Confronts the Six Headwinds* (No. w18315). Cambridge: National Bureau of Economic Research.

Gould, S. J. (1987). The Panda's Thumb of Technology. *Natural History*, 1, 14-23.

Grabher, G. (1993). Rediscovering the Social in the Economies of Interfirm Relations. In Grabher, G. (Eds.). *The Embedded Firm: On the Socioeconomics of Industrial Networks* (pp. 255-277). London: Routledge.

Grillitsch, M., & Nilsson, M. (2015). Innovation in peripheral regions: Do collaborations compensate for a lack of local knowledge spillovers?. *The Annals of Regional Science, 54*(1), 299-321.

Grupo de Memoria Histórica. (2016). *Informe General Grupo de Memoria Histórica*. Bogotá: Comisión Nacional de Reparación y Reconciliación.

Gutiérrez, L. F. (2008). Salir de las Fronteras. *El Espectador*. 25 May 2008. Retrieved from https://www.elespectador.com/node/15831/

Hambleton, R. (2015). Power, place and the new civic leadership. *Local Economy, 30*(2), 167-172.

Headrick, D. R. (1988). *The Tentacles of Progress: Technology Transfer in the Age of Imperialism, 1850-1940*. New York: Oxford University Press.

Helmsing, A. H. J. (1990). Cambio Económico y Desarrollo Regional. Bogotá: CIDER Universidad De Los Andes.

Hermelin, M. (1996). Geologia y Paisaje. In Melo, J. O. (Eds.). Historia de Medellín: Tomo I (pp. 3-16). Bogotá: Compañía Suramericana de Seguros.

Hidalgo, C. A., Klinger, B., Barabási, A. L., & Hausmann, R. (2007). The product space conditions the development of nations. *Science, 317*(5837), 482-487.

Himanen, P. (2010). *The Hacker Ethic*. New York: Random House.

Hirsch, J. (2015). Elon Musk's Growing Empire is fueled by $4.9 Billon in Government Subsidies. *Los Angeles Times*. Retrieved from https://www.latimes.com/business/la-fi-hy-musk-subsidies-20150531-story.html

Howells, J. R. (2006). Intermediation and the Role of Intermediaries in Innovation. *Research Policy, 35*(5), 715-728.

Huuhtanen, M. (2015). Why Europe isn't creating any Googles or Facebooks. *Business Insider*. Retrieved from https://www.businessinsider.com/ap-why-europe-isnt-creating-any-googles-or-facebooks-2015-9

Hylton, F. (2007). Medellín's Makeover. *New Left Review, 44*, 70-89.

Iammarino, S. (2005). An Evolutionary Integrated View of Regional Systems of Innovation: Concepts, Measures and Historical Perspectives. *European Planning Studies, 13*(4), 497-519.

Iammarino, S., Rodríguez-Pose, A., & Storper, M. (2017). Why regional development matters for Europe's economic future. Retrieved from http://ec.europa.eu/regional_policy/sources/docgener/work/201707_region al_development_matters.pdf

Islam, N. (2003). What Have we Learnt from the Convergence Debate?. *Journal of Economic Surveys, 17*(3), 309-362.

Josephson, P. R. (1995). Projects of the Century in Soviet History: Large-Scale Technologies from Lenin to Gorbachev. *Technology and Culture, 36*(3), 519-559.

Kalmanovitz, S., & López E. (2006). *La Agricultura Colombiana en el Siglo XX*. Mexico City: Fondo de Cultura Económica.

Keller, W. (2004). International Technology Diffusion. *Journal of Economic Literature, 42*(3),752-782.

Knight, R. V. (1995). Knowledge-Based Development: Policy and Planning Implications for Cities. *Urban studies, 32*(2), 225-260.

Kondratieff. N. D. (1984). *The long wave cycle*. New York: Richardson & Snyder.

Koonin, E. V., & Wolf, Y. I. (2009). Is Evolution Darwinian or/and Lamarckian?. *Biology direct, 4*(1), 42.

Lach, S. (2002). Do R&D subsidies stimulate or displace private R&D? Evidence from Israel. *Journal of Industrial Economics, 50*(4), 369-390.

Lamb, R. D. (2010). *Microdynamics of Illegitimacy and Complex Urban Violence in Medellín, Colombia*. PhD Dissertation. Maryland: University of Maryland.

Lambooy, J. G., & Boschma, R. A. (2001). Evolutionary Economics and Regional Policy. *The Annals of Regional Science, 35*(1), 113-131.

Landes, D. S. (1998). *The Wealth and Poverty of Nations: Why Some Are So Rich and Others So Poor*. New York City: W. W. Norton.

Lane, P. (1996). The Other Medellín Cartel. *Business Week*. 56-58.

Laranja, M., Uyarra, E. and Flanagan, K. (2008). Policies for Science, Technology and Innovation: Translating Rationales into Regional Policies in a Multilevel Setting. *Research Policy, 37*(5), 823–835.

Lazarsfeld, P., Berelson, B., & Gaudet, H. (1944). *The People's Choice*. New York: Duell, Sloan and Pearce.

Lerner, J. (2009). *Boulevard of Broken Dreams: Why Public Efforts to Boost Entrepreneurship and Venture Capital Have Failed—and What to Do About It*. Princeton: Princeton University Press.

Levine, M. E., & Forrence, J. L. (1990). Regulatory Capture, Public Interest, and the Public Agenda: Toward a Synthesis. *Journal of Law, Economics, & Organization, 6*, 167-198.

Life. (1947). MEDELLÍN: South American Showplace is Hailed as a "Capitalist Paradise. *LIFE Magazine.* 109-117.

List, F. (1856). *National System of Political Economy.* Philadelphia: J. B. Lippincott & Company.

Londoño, C. F. (2004). Grupo Empresarial Antioqueño: evolución de políticas y estrategias, 1978-2002. *Revista eia,* (1), 47-62.

Lundvall, B. Å. (1992). *National Systems of Innovation: Towards a Theory of Innovation and Interactive Learning.* London: Pinter.

Maclean, K. (2014). *The 'Medellín Miracle': The Politics of Crisis, Elites and Coalitions.* Birmingham: Development Leadership Program, University of Birmingham.

Malecki, E. J. (1997). *Technology and Economic Development: The Dynamics of Local, Regional, and National Change.* New York: Longman Scientific & Technical.

Marques, P. & Morgan, K. (2018). The Heroic Assumptions of Smart Specialisation: A Sympathetic Critique of Regional Innovation Policy. In Isaksen, A., Martin, R., & Trippl, M. (Eds.). *New Avenues for Regional Innovation Systems - Theoretical Advances, Empirical Cases and Policy Lessons.* New York: Springer.

Marshall, A. (1890). *Principles of Economics: An Introductory Volume.* London: Macmillan.

Martin, G. (2012). *Medellín Tragedia y Resurreccion: Mafia, Ciudad y Estado, 1975-2012.* Bogotá: Planeta.

Maskell, P., & Malmberg, A. (1999a). Localised Learning and Industrial Competitiveness. *Cambridge Journal of Economics, 23*(2), 167-185.

Maskell, P., & Malmberg, A. (1999b). The Competitiveness of Firms and Regions 'Ubiquitification'and the Importance of Localized Learning. *European Urban and Regional Studies, 6*(1), 9-25.

Mazzucato, M. (2013). *The entrepreneurial state: Debunking the public vs. private myth in risk and innovation*. London: Anthem.

Mazzucato, M. (2018). Mission-oriented innovation policies: challenges and opportunities. *Industrial and Corporate Change, 27*(5), 803-815.

Mendonça, S., Pereira, T. S., & Godinho, M. M. (2004). Trademarks as an indicator of innovation and industrial change. *Research Policy, 33*(9), 1385-1404.

Metcalfe, J. S. (2005) Evolutionary Concepts in Relation to Evolutionary Economics. In Dopfer, K. (Eds.*). The Evolutionary Foundations of Economics* (pp. 391–430). Cambridge: Cambridge University Press.

Metcalfe, J. S., & Ramlogan, R. (2008). Innovation Systems and the Competitive Process in Developing Economies. *The Quarterly Review of Economics and Finance, 48*(2), 433-446.

Miller, R. E., & Cote, M. (1987). Growing the next Silicon Valley: A guide for successful regional planning. New York: Free Press.

Mokyr, J. (1990). *The Lever of Riches: Technological Creativity and Economic Progress*. New York: Oxford University Press.

Molina Londoño, L. F. (1996). La Economia Local en el Siglo XIX. In Melo, J. O. (Eds.). *Historia de Medellín: Tomo I* (pp. 201-213). Bogotá: Compañía Suramericana de Seguros.

Moncada, E. (2016). Urban Violence, Political Economy, and Territorial Control: Insights from Medellín. *Latin American Research Review, 51*(4), 225-248.

Moreno, R., Paci, R. & Usai, S. (2005). Spatial Spillovers and Innovation Activity in European Regions. *Environment and Planning A, 37*,1793–1812.

Morisson, A. (2019). Innovation centres as anchor spaces of the 'knowledge city'. *Global Business and Economics Review, 21*(3/4), 330–345

Morisson, A., & Bevilacqua, C. (2018). Balancing gentrification in the knowledge economy: the case of Chattanooga's innovation district. *Urban Research & Practice*, 1-21.

Morrison, A., Rabellotti, R., & Zirulia, L. (2013). When Do Global Pipelines Enhance the Diffusion of Knowledge in Clusters?. *Economic Geography*, *89*(1), 77-96.

Murrell, P. (1993). What is shock therapy? What did it do in Poland and Russia?. *Post-Soviet Affairs*, *9*(2), 111-140.

Myrdal, G. (1957). *Economic Theory and Underdeveloped Regions*. London: Duckworth.

Narula, R. (2004). *Understanding Absorptive Capacities in an Innovation Systems Context: Consequences for Economic and Employment Growth*. DRUID Working Paper no. 04–02, December. Maastricht: MERIT.

Nearshore Americas. (2015). HP Abandons Medellín Global Center and Has No One to Blame But Itself. *Nearshore Americas*. June 11, 2015. Retrieved from http://www.nearshoreamericas.com/hp-kills-Medellín-global-services-center-blame/

Neffke, F., Henning, M., & Boschma, R. (2011). How do regions diversify over time? Industry relatedness and the development of new growth paths in regions. *Economic Geography, 87*(3), 237-265.

Nelson, R. R. (1993). *National Innovation Systems: A Comparative Analysis*. New York: Oxford University Press.

Nelson, R. R., & Winter, S. G. (1982). *An Evolutionary Theory of Economic Change*. Boston: Harvard University Press.

Nooteboom, B., & Stam, E. (2008). *Micro-Foundations for Innovation Policy*. Amsterdam: Amsterdam University Press.

North, D. C. (1990). *Institutions, Institutional Change and Economic Performance*. Cambridge: Cambridge University Press.

O'Brien, R. (1992). *Global Financial Integration: The End of Geography*. London: Royal Institute of International Affairs.

OCyT. (2018). Principales indicadores de inversión en actividades de ciencia, tecnología e innovación. Retrieved from http://ocyt.org.co/portal-de-datos-abiertos/indicadores-grupos-de-investigacion/

OECD. (2005). *Oslo Manual-Guidelines for Collecting and Interpreting Innovation Data*. Paris: OECD Publishing.

OECD. (2006). *Competitive Cities in the Global Economy*. Paris: OECD Publishing. European Commission. (2018). Available budget 2014-2020. Retrieved from http://ec.europa.eu/regional_policy/en/funding/available-budget/

OECD. (2011a). *Regions and Innovation Policy,* OECD Reviews of Regional Innovation. Paris: OECD Publishing.

OECD. (2011b). *OECD Regional Outlook 2011*: *Building resilient regions for stronger economies*. Paris: OECD Publishing.

OECD. (2015a). *Promoting the Development of Local Innovation Systems: The Case of Medellín, Colombia*. Trento: OECD LEED Publishing.

OECD. (2015b). *The Innovation Imperative: Contributing to Productivity, Growth and Well-Being*. Paris: OECD Publishing.

Ohmae, K. (1995). *The End of the Nation State: The Rise of Regional Economies*. London: Harper Collins.

Ortiz Mesa, L. J. (1996). Viajeros y Forasteros en Medellín, siglos XIX y XX. In Melo, J. O. (Eds.). *Historia de Medellín: Tomo* I (pp. 289-304). Bogotá: Compañía Suramericana de Seguros.

Oughton, C., Landabaso, M., & Morgan, K. (2002). The regional innovation paradox: innovation policy and industrial policy. *The Journal of Technology Transfer, 27*(1), 97-110.

Owen-Smith, J., & Powell, W. W. (2004). Knowledge Networks as Channels and Conduits: The Effects of Spillovers in the Boston Biotechnology Community. *Organization Science, 15*(1), 5-21.

Palacios, M. (2006). *Between Legitimacy and Violence: A History of Colombia, 1875–2002*. Durham: Duke University Press.

Perez, C. (2010). Technological Revolutions and Technological Paradigms. *Cambridge Journal of Economics, 34*(1), 185–202.

Piedrahita Echeverri, J. (1988). *Documentos y Estudios para la Historia de Medellín*. Medellín: Concejo de Medellín.

Pike, A., Coombes, M., O'Brien, P., & Tomaney, J. (2018). Austerity states, institutional dismantling and the governance of sub-national economic development: The demise of the regional development agencies in England. *Territory, Politics, Governance*, 6(1), 118-144.

Pineda, L. & Scheel, C. (2011). *Plan de Ciencia, Tecnología e Innovación de Medellín -2010*. Medellín: Ruta N.

Polanyi, K. (1957). *The Great Transformation*. Boston: Beacon Press.

Polanyi, M. (1966). *The Tacit Dimension*. London: Routledge & Kegan Paul.

Pollitt, C., Talbot, C., Caulfield, J., & Smullen, A. (2004). Agencies: How governments do things through semiautonomous organizations. Basingstoke: Palgrave/Macmillan.

Poveda Ramos, G. (1996). Industrialización y Economía, 1890-1950. In Melo, J. O. (Eds.). *Historia de Medellín: Tomo I* (pp. 307-325). Bogotá: Compañía Suramericana de Seguros.

Poveda Ramos, G. (2011). *Ingenieros y Científicos Inmigrantes a Colombia 1760-1950*. Medellín: Gobernación de Antioquia.

Ramírez Moreno, H. (2006). *Descentralización y Desarrollo Institucional en Colombia: Análisis Crítico*. Ibagué: Universidad del Tolima.

Rantisi, N. M. (2002). The Local Innovation System as a Source of 'Variety': Openness and Adaptability in New York City's Garment District. *Regional Studies*, 36(6), 587-602.

Ray, G. F. (1980). Innovation as the Source of Long Term Economic Growth. *Long Range Planning*, 13(2), 9-19.

Restrepo Santamaria, N. (2011). *Empresariado Antioqueño y Sociedad, 1940-2004: Influencia de las Elites Patronales de Antioquia en las Políticas Socioeconómica*. Medellín: Editorial Universidad de Antioquia.

Restrepo Uribe, J. (1981). *Medellín, Su Origen, Progreso, y Desarrollo*. Medellín: Servigraficas.

Restrepo, O. L. (1992). El Enigma de las Masacres en Medellín. *El Tiempo*. Retrieved from http://www.eltiempo.com/archivo/documento/MAM-35942

Rodríguez-Pose, A. (2018). The revenge of the places that don't matter (and what to do about it). *Cambridge Journal of Regions, Economy and Society*, *11*(1), 189-209.

Rodríguez-Pose, A., & Crescenzi, R. (2008a). Mountains in a Flat World: Why Proximity Still Matters for the Location of Economic Activity. *Cambridge Journal of Regions, Economy and Society*, *1*(3), 371-388.

Rodriguez-Pose, A., & Crescenzi, R. (2008b). R&D, Spillovers, Innovation Systems and the Genesis of Regional Growth in Europe. *Regional Studies*, *42*(1), 51-67.

Rodrik, D. (2006). Goodbye Washington consensus, hello Washington confusion? A review of the World Bank's economic growth in the 1990s: learning from a decade of reform. *Journal of Economic literature*, *44*(4), 973-987.

Rodrik, D. (2008). *One Economics, Many Recipes: Globalization, Institutions, and Economic Growth*. Princeton: Princeton University Press.

Romer, P. M. (1994). The Origins of Endogenous Growth. *The Journal of Economic Perspectives*, *8*(1), 3-22.

Romero, S. (2007). Medellín's nonconformist mayor turns blight to beauty. *New York Times*. Retrieved from http://www.nytimes.com/2007/07/15/world/americas/15Medellín.html?pagewanted=all&_r=0

Rosen, S. (1981). The Economics of Superstars. *The American Economic Review*, *71*(5), 845-858.

Rosenberg, N. (1982). *Inside the Black Box: Technology and Economics*. Cambridge: Cambridge University Press.

Rosenthal, S. S., & Strange, W. C. (2004). Evidence on the Nature and Sources of Agglomeration Economies. *Handbook of Regional and Urban Economics*, *4*, 2119-2171.

Rosenthal, S. S., & Strange, W. C. (2005). The geography of entrepreneurship in the New York metropolitan area. *Federal Reserve Bank of New York Economic Policy Review, 11*(2), 29-54.

Ruta N. (2010a). Informe de Gestión 2010. Retrieved from http://www.rutanMedellín.org/es/nosotros/ruta-n/informes-de-gestion

Ruta N. (2010b). Cumpleaños de Ruta N: hablan sus artifices. [Video file]. Retrieved from https://www.youtube.com/watch?v=BcWqa9p6Deg

Ruta N. (2013). Ingresos, costos y utilidades en emprendimientos digitales. Retrieved from https://www.rutanMedellín.org//es/actualidad/noticias/item/ingresos-costos-y-utilidades-en-emprendimientos-digitales-20082019

Ruta N. (2014). *Qué es Innovación y cuál es su Impacto Socio-Económico.* Medellín: Corporación Ruta n Medellín.

Ruta N. (2015). ¿Qué es el Plan CT+i de Ruta N? [Video file]. Retrieved from https://www.youtube.com/watch?v=Q94E3yqUdb4&index=102&list=WL

Ruta N. (2016). Informe de Gestión 2014. Retrieved from http://www.rutanMedellín.org/es/nosotros/ruta-n/informes-de-gestion

Ruta N. (2018a). Informe de Gestión 2018. Retrieved from http://www.rutanMedellín.org/es/nosotros/ruta-n/informes-de-gestion

Ruta N. (2018b). Medellín es la ciudad que más invierte en innovación en Colombia. Retrieved from https://www.rutanMedellín.org/es/noticias-rutan/item/medell%C3%ADn-es-la-ciudad-que-m%C3%A1s-invierte-en-innovaci%C3%B3n-en-colombia

Salazar, A. (1990). *No Nacimos pa' Semilla.* Bogotá: CINEP.

Samper, L. (2012). 400 jobs expected by 2014 with Hewlett Packard Global Center in Medellín: Minister Díaz-Granados. September 19, 2012. Retrieved from http://www.mincit.gov.co/englishmin/publicaciones/4395/400_jobs_expec ted_by_2014_with_hewlett_packard_global_center_in_Medellín_minister _diaz-granados

Sánchez Mejía, M. (2011). La Estrategia de Regionalización del Sistema Nacional de Ciencia y Tecnología como Parte del Proceso de Descentralización en Colombia. *Cuadernos de Administración*, *15*(22), 107-116.

Sassen, S. (2001). *The Global City: New York, London, Tokyo*. Princeton: Princeton University Press.

Saxenian, A. (1994). *Regional Advantage: Culture and Competition in Silicon Valley and Route 128*. Cambridge: Harvard University Press.

Schipani, A. (2014). Colombia's Sindicato Antioqueño has Become a Force for the Country's Good. *Financial Times*. Retrieved from https://www.ft.com/content/3b95966a-a61b-11e3-8a2a-00144feab7de?mhq5j=e7

Schot, J., & Steinmueller, W. E. (2018). Three frames for innovation policy: R&D, systems of innovation and transformative change. *Research Policy*, *47*(9), 1554-1567.

Schumpeter, J. A. (1939). *Business cycles*. New York: McGraw-Hill.

Schwab, K. (2016). *The Fourth Industrial Revolution*. Geneva: The World Economic Forum.

Semana. (2011). El Silicon Valley Paisa. *Semana,* September, 17, 2011. Retrieved from http://www.semana.com/economia/articulo/el-silicon-valley-paisa/246492-3

SIC. (2018). Estadísticas Propriedad Industrial. Retrieved from http://www.sic.gov.co/estadisticas-propiedad-industrial

Smith, K. (2000). Innovation as a Systemic Phenomenon: Rethinking the Role of Policy. *Enterprise and Innovation Management Studies*, *1*(1), 73-102.

Solow, R. M. (1957). Technical change and the aggregate production function. *The Review of Economics and Statistics*, *39*, 312-320.

Storper, M., & Venables, A. J. (2004). Buzz: Face-to-Face Contact and the Urban Economy. *Journal of Economic Geography*, *4*(4), 351-370.

Storper, M., Kemeny, T., Makarem, N., & Osman, T. (2015). *The Rise and Fall of Urban Economies: Lessons from San Francisco and Los Angeles*. Palo Alto: Stanford University Press.

Sturgeon, T. J. (2000). How Silicon Valley came to be. In Kenney, M. (2000). *Understanding Silicon Valley: Anatomy of an Entrepreneurial Region* (pp. 15-47). Palo Alto: Stanford University Press.

The Economist. (2001). Business Looks Outwards. *The Economist*. Retrieved from http://www.economist.com/node/576270

The State Council. (2017). China issues guideline on artificial intelligence development. Retrieved from http://english.gov.cn/policies/latest_releases/2017/07/20/content_2814757 42458322.html

Tödtling, F., & Trippl, M. (2005). One size fits all?: Towards a differentiated regional innovation policy approach. *Research policy*, *34*(8), 1203-1219.

U.S. Census. (2018). GINI Index of Income Inequality. Retrieved from https://factfinder.census.gov/faces/tableservices/jsf/pages/productview.xht ml?pid=ACS_17_5YR_B19083&prodType=table

US Embassy. (2008). Confidential Cables id: 167730 and id: 182470. Retrieved from http://static.iris.net.co/semana/upload/documents/Doc-2258_20111010.pdf

Utterback, J. M. (1994). *Mastering the Dynamics of Innovation: How Companies Can Seize Opportunities in the Face of Technological Change*. Boston: Harvard Business School Press.

Valencia Restrepo, J. (1996). La Industrialización de Medellín y su Area Circundante. In Melo, J. O. (Eds.). *Historia de Medellín: Tomo II* (pp. 476-486). Bogotá: Compañía Suramericana de Seguros.

Veblen, T. (1898). Why is Economics not an Evolutionary Science?. *The Quarterly Journal of Economics*, *12*(4), 373-397.

Verhoest, K., Van Thiel, S., Bouckaert, G., & Laegreid, P. (2012). Government Agencies: Practices and LessonsFrom 30 Countries. Basingstoke: Palgrave Macmillan.

Von Hippel, E. (1994). "Sticky Information" and the Locus of Problem Solving: Implications for Innovation. *Management science, 40*(4), 429-439.

Wade, R. (1990). *Governing the market: Economic theory and the role of government in East Asian industrialization.* Princeton: Princeton University Press.

Wall Street Journal. (2013). The City of the Year. *The Wall Street Journal.* Retrieved from http://online.wsj.com/ad/cityoftheyear

Williamson, J. (2002). Did the Washington Consensus Fail? *PIIE.* Retrieved from https://piie.com/commentary/speeches-papers/did-washington-consensus-fail

Woolthuis, R. K., Lankhuizen, M., & Gilsing, V. (2005). A System Failure Framework for Innovation Policy Design. *Technovation, 25*(6), 609-619.

World Bank. (2018). World Bank Open Data. Retrieved from https://data.worldbank.org/

Zhou, P., & Leydesdorff, L. (2006). The Emergence of China as a Leading Nation in Science. *Research Policy, 35*(1), 83-104.